# RISE UP!
## The Keys to Ultimate Dental Practice Success

Colin Receveur

CEO, SmartBox

"As we started to look around to see who could do marketing for us and who actually understood dentists, there wasn't really anybody else out there ... it worked out beautifully when we looked into SmartBox."

— **Dr. Lynette Crouse, Houston, Texas**

"I was looking for a company that knew what high-quality dental marketing was. Over the years, I've dealt with probably three to four different companies before I moved to SmartBox. I visited with Colin, and it was obvious from my conversation with him, and his family background, that he understood dentistry, and that he knew what needed to be done to promote a dental practice appropriately and effectively. I've been very happy with the results that we've received with SmartBox."

— **Dr. Dick Davenport, Laredo, Texas**

"I've had other companies represent me on the internet, and usually it's done by phone. An interview real quick, and they throw something together that's probably like twenty other websites out there. I felt like SmartBox has really tried to get to know me the best that they can through different questionnaires but mostly through talking to me over the phone, visiting me in my hometown, and seeing what the demographics are here, and so I think that they've certainly been the most thorough."

— **Dr. David Porter, Gillette, Wyoming**

"I think the fact that Colin's experience watching his dad in practice and then being able to have that first-hand knowledge really makes a big difference for somebody promoting dental marketing services. And so that, I think, was a big attractor for me. He understood the market that he was trying to serve, and he had an insider's take on it, so to speak."
— **Dr. Scott Watterson, Jackson, Michigan**

"Colin Receveur is the real deal! He delivers results on time and every time! I highly recommend Colin for all your targeted patient acquisition leads."
—**Dr. Ivan Terrero, Bonita Springs, Florida**

Matthew 7:24-27 from THE HOLY BIBLE, NEW
INTERNATIONAL VERSION®, NIV® Copyright © 1973, 1978,
1984, 2011 by Biblica, Inc.™ Used by permission. All rights
reserved worldwide.

"You keep using that word. I do not think it
means what you think it means,"
from *The Princess Bride*, 20th Century Fox, 1987.

For permissions or more information, please write to:
**SmartBox**
821 Mount Tabor Road, Suite 300, New Albany, IN 47150
Phone: 502.509.1413
Fax: 502.371.0659

colin@smartboxdentalmarketing.com
www.smartboxdentalmarketing.com
Facebook: www.fb.me/SmartBoxWebMarketing
Twitter: @creceveur
YouTube: www.youtube.com/SmartBoxWeb


Published and printed in the United States of America

To my dad, Ron Receveur, DDS,
who at first tolerated and later fully
supported my love of all things internet.
Somewhere out there, Dad,
there's a saint who wants his patience back.

# CONTENTS

# FOREWORD

When the people at SmartBox contacted me and told me that Colin was writing a new book, I was excited to hear it.

You see, when it comes to dental marketing, Colin Receveur is the real deal.

There is no smoke and mirrors. He walks the walk.

Son of a dentist. That's a great start. Dentistry is in his blood. Colin knows dentistry. He knows what dentists go through. He understands how dentists work and how they think.

Don't let those boyish good looks deceive you. Colin has been around in dentistry for a long time. I've known Colin now for over eight years, and in every one of those years, he has taken SmartBox from strength to strength to strength.

More importantly, Colin knows marketing. He knows how and where to find you those new patients. He knows how to attract those new patients to your office, and how to nurture that initial relationship with those new patients so that they feel welcomed, trusted, and understood.

It's no accident that Colin Receveur and SmartBox are the go-to people when it comes to building your dental practice. Every dental practice needs a healthy supply of new patient enquiries.

Colin and his team know the formulas you need to use to have those new patients beating a path to your dental office front door.

When Colin titled this book, he approached me because he felt that as the inventor of the Ultimate Patient Experience™, I might have felt a little slighted by his use of the word "ultimate" in the title. On the contrary, I was delighted to see Colin describe this book in that way. Because there is no better word that could be used here; "ultimate" is the perfect fit.

I work with dentists to help them with the systems that they need to keep and retain their patients. Colin and SmartBox help dentists to attract and convert more new patients into those dental offices. It is a perfect match.

I'm excited about this book, and I'm looking forward to seeing the growth of the dental offices that apply the principles and systems that are explained on the pages inside.

This book is a game-changer. Read it once, and then reread it. Then read it again. Highlight it. Write in it. Bend the corners of the pages.

But most importantly, use the information inside this book. Put the ideas and concepts into action in your dental office.

These ideas are not theories. They are tried and proven.

You owe it to yourself and to your family to build the best possible dental office that you can.

And you owe it to the people of your community that they find out about you, because you are the best dentist around.

The ideas in this book will make sure that more people find you.

*David Moffet.*

Dr. David Moffet, BDS, FPFA, CSP

Author of the #1 Amazon Bestseller *How to Build the Dental Practice of Your Dreams (Without Killing Yourself!) in Less Than 60 Days*

david@theUPE.com
www.theUltimatePatientExperience.com
www.BuildingYourDreamPractice.com

# FIRST THOUGHTS

The "Golden Age of Dentistry" lasted from the end of the Second World War until roughly 1970. By some reports, what brought that age to an end was, in part, fluoridated water.

Prior to fluoridation of the public water supplies, dentists spent an estimated 41 percent of their time filling cavities. By 1982, an astonishing **27 percent** of kids under 18 were cavity-free. That was a serious hit to dentists' incomes.

A 1982 article by Jerry Berger quoted one dentist who'd managed to put **eight kids through college** during the Golden Age—while also acquiring a summer home on Cape Cod and a sailboat. That dentist was pretty well set for retirement, too.

There's no way of knowing whether that doctor was typical for the time. What is certain, though, is that the landscape of dentistry has changed dramatically and will continue to change going forward.

I'm not talking technology, although a typical dentist from the 1970s would be amazed at what doctors today have at their disposal. I'm talking about people.

People are far more mobile now than they were 40 or even 30 years ago. You simply can't count on a significant percentage of your existing patients remaining your patients. Families relocate far too often these days.

Moreover, what worked for dentists in the 1970s through the 1990s to get enough new patients simply doesn't work well enough today. It's a brave new world of dental marketing that is equal parts bewildering and troublesome for many dentists.

And more dentists are operating in this country now than at any other time in history. Competition is fierce, and it's only going to get worse.

I'm not going to belabor the woes that beset dentists on every side today. You know them and you live them, probably every day. What I am going to tell you is that for most dentists today, things are worse than they seem.

This isn't a doom-and-gloom message. **It's a message of hope**. The problems facing dentists are severe, but they can be overcome by using the approach outlined in this book. That's why I wrote it—I've made it my life's mission to help dentists succeed. That's also the reason I founded SmartBox—to help dentists **thrive**.

I know that I can't help all dentists. Some are just too set in their ways and unwilling to make the mental leap and do what it takes to attract not only more patients, but better patients as well.

I hope you're not one of them. The fact that you purchased this book (and that you're actually reading it) suggests that you want better than you're getting now.

Read on, doctor, and my best wishes for your ultimate success.

Keep Moving Forward,

**"I felt that Colin and his
company take care of
everything to a level
that I just had to say, listen:
If I'm serious about this,
I've got to take
this leap of faith.
And I'm very happy
that I did."**

— Dr. David Bistritz, Aventura, Florida

# BEING BUSY DOESN'T CUT IT ANYMORE

*It's not enough to be busy; so are the ants.
The question is:
What are we busy about?*
~ Henry David Thoreau

" I have four kids and a wife and we're all busy, but sometimes being busy practicing dentistry is not what I want to be busy doing. I coach soccer, I am involved with my kids' lives, I value my marriage and we spend a lot of time together, but not enough. And so, at the end of the day, at the end of life, I want to be able to look back and say I spent the time I needed to with those that mattered most. And so, focusing on dentistry that frees up my time to be out of the office more is a huge thing, and that's really where I feel SmartBox is going to make a big difference in my practice moving forward."
— **Dr. Scott Watterson, Jackson, Michigan**

I was talking with a dentist from the Northwest the other day. Nice guy, and a pretty savvy businessman from what I could tell. During our conversation, I asked him how things were going.

"We're really busy," he told me.

I congratulated him, and then asked kind of a stupid/smart question. "Are you making any money?"

"Not nearly as much as I'd like," he answered.

"Why not?"

"We're seeing a lot of our longtime patients moving away," he said. "That was an ongoing revenue stream I could count on, but now it's drying up. The new patients I'm getting are looking for the least amount of dentistry at the lowest price. And then they're gone. There's no loyalty to our practice."

"But that's probably happening with your competition too, isn't it?" I asked.

He laughed, with a tinge of bitterness. "You mean all my established competitors plus the three others that have opened in the last 18 months? You wouldn't believe all the low-price offers that are flying around. I'm cutting margins more than I ever have."

Unfortunately, he was wrong; I believed every word, and I'm going to tell you why. Bear with me for the next few pages; let's get the bad news out of the way, then it's all the good news.

# The Traditional Model for Dental Practices Is Dead ... or at Least the Walking Dead

The days of the one-dentist office are numbered, and the same may hold true for the two-dentist practice. The halcyon days of a dentist setting up shop and treating most of his or her patients for decades are past.

The United States has a very mobile population. Relocations within towns, counties, and states, and relocation to other states, is common. Common enough, in fact, that an entire *enormous* industry has grown up around "relo" services—more than $25 billion, by some estimates. That's not just moving companies; the industry also includes home-finding services, relocation coordinators, and much more.

If you need any proof that the relocation business is in great shape, let me ask you: When was the last time you heard about a national moving company going broke? Business is booming because people are moving.

High geographic mobility means the constant loss of established patients from a given market. And when I say high, I mean in the tens of millions of people a year. From 2016-2017, nearly 37 million people in the U.S. relocated.

Of those 37 million, 21 million (58 percent) relocated within the same county, which on the face of it doesn't sound too bad. But that doesn't mean you'll keep your existing patients who relocate.

Convenience and proximity matter to a lot of people, particularly to busy families with children. In large counties and heavily populated urban areas, travel time is a serious consideration. If your existing patient moves five to ten miles away from your practice, and another dentist is more conveniently located to work or school, that patient is probably gone.

Of course, new-to-you prospects may move into your market as well. All things being equal, which they hardly ever are, you might get fewer patients overall, or more new patients, depending on the real estate market dynamics in your area.

Which outcome you experience—new patient loss or growth—will depend a great deal on your online presence.

# The Road to Today's Dentist Begins Online

More than 90 percent of dental prospects begin their search for a dentist online. The internet has revolutionized the process of attracting new patients. People have more choice and more access to information (literally at their fingertips) than ever before. Finding a new dentist is easier than at any other time in history.

That ease of investigating active dentists in a given area can work for or against you, depending on how your online presence stacks up against your competitors. If your dental website is on the second or third page of local search results—and today, all search is local—the odds are high that prospects will choose another dentist before ever seeing your marketing.

If your website takes more than three seconds to load, those prospects will click away.

If your website doesn't display properly across multiple devices—desktop and laptop computers, tablets, and *particularly* smartphones—they're gone.

Did you know that today more searches are conducted from mobile devices than from desktop and laptop computers? Mobile searches took the lead in 2016 and have been steadily pulling ahead ever since.

> One of the things that I really felt is that with my generation, when you see a billboard or you see a TV commercial, what do you do? You Google that thing, and you look it up. Our website was not mobile-friendly. That's when we switched to SmartBox, because SmartBox could make our website mobile-friendly.
> — **Dr. Katie Post, Rochester, Minnesota**

Bottom line: Your prospects expect **an excellent and seamless online experience**, and they'll leave quickly if they don't get it.

Make no mistake: When those prospects are gone, they're *gone*. They'll choose another doctor to solve their dental problems.

Those two factors alone—a highly mobile population and the ease of locating a new dentist—can erode your patient base, but the situation is actually worse than that. There are other factors at play here.

## Here Come the New Dentists ... and the Dental Corporations

Competition for new dental patients is increasing on several fronts.

A record number of dental schools are graduating record numbers of new dentists with record levels of debt. Today, the **average** educational debt for a new dentist is a staggering **$260,000**. Dental school debt can easily run to more than $300,000 or much more … and in fact, that higher figure holds for 30 percent of graduates.

To say that those new doctors are eager to get to work is an understatement. And there are a lot of them.

The graduating dental school class of 2016 had 5,957 graduates, up from 5,811 in 2015. Total predoctoral enrollment is currently at its highest level ever, with nearly 25,000 students enrolled in the 2016-17 academic year.

The number of new dentists is forecast to increase by at least 500 per year by 2020. Again, that doesn't sound too bad until you consider that not all of those graduates will be distributed equally among markets. If you're in a relatively small market, what would two new dental practices do to your bottom line?

Even in a larger market, a single new dental practice that's geographically close to yours can lead to loss of new patients, and even some of your existing patients.

However, it's not only new graduates opening practices that you need to watch. Those debt-laden new dentists are fuel for the corporate dentistry machine.

Corporate dentistry, also referred to as dental management organizations (DMOs), is entering more and more markets and employing more and more of those new dentists. It's a sweet deal for a new dentist, who can realize huge sign-on bonuses (a recent offer from Aspen Dental was $30,000 just to sign) and even tuition repayment ($200,000 sounds awfully good to a new dentist). Not only that, but graduates can get right to work making a very attractive salary—almost certainly in the $120,000-$130,000 range, and even higher in some areas.

With a ready supply of new talent, corporate chains are eager to expand, and many of them are. Aspen Dental, for instance, states that it has added 60 or more practices every year since 2014. Aspen projected that it would add 75 new corporate practices in 2017, bringing its total to 675. That might not sound so bad, but Aspen is projecting it will **double** the number of practices in the next five years.

And that's just one dental chain.

If you've been paying attention, this probably doesn't come as a shock. The arc of corporate dentistry has been long, but the trajectory is set and the process is accelerating.

Here's a post that appeared on our SmartBox blog in October 2016. Even then, the direction that corporate dentistry was taking was clear.

## Is All the Hype About Corporate Dentistry True?

The penetration of corporate dentistry into different markets in the U.S. is uneven. In fact, it may not have reached your market yet. Where corporate dentistry has reached, the effects are becoming clearer.

An article published in May of this year described the growing impact of corporate dentistry in Texas.

In addition to a "major" presence at the state dental association annual meeting, well-known chains such as Heartland Dental are affecting the career paths of newly graduated dentists.

The "traditional" path for a new dentist led in one of two directions: acquire the financing and operating capital to open a new practice or purchase an existing one; or work as an associate for an established dentist to gain experience and startup capital.

With dental school tuition having soared in the last decade, more and more new graduates are choosing to delay solopreneurship and to work for corporate chains. Many of them are reluctant to add more indebtedness to an already staggering student loan debt.

## Feeding the Machine

The article also noted that corporate chains are becoming very aggressive in trying to acquire individual practices from retiring dentists. Typically, the purchase includes a stipulation that the dentist remains on for a period of time to ensure continuity and that the patient base remains loyal.

If there are fewer new dental school grads looking to acquire an existing practice, retirement-ready dentists have only two options: keep working until they locate a buyer, or sell to corporate entities.

The aggressive approach appears to be working; the article also notes that the major chains in Texas are, for the first time, turning to external staffing services to locate talent for their offices.

# Will the Texas Experience Generalize?

Markets are different, and undoubtedly, some don't hold sufficient promise to attract a strong corporate dentistry presence. But the chains' playbook seems clear: establish a presence, acquire existing practices to reduce competition, and attract a significant number of new dentists to staff the offices. The new graduates appear to be okay with the prospect, which undoubtedly reflects a pragmatic approach of making a living and paying down debt.

A strong corporate dentistry presence won't prevent motivated "dentalpreneurs" from opening new practices, but it's certain to give many of them pause. In the long run, the presence of the chains may discourage lenders from funding new practices, but that remains to be seen.

For existing practices, the presence of the dental chains is rarely good news. Corporate dentistry's economies of scale in terms of purchasing, negotiating rents, and handling HR and payroll puts small dental practices at a competitive disadvantage. Additionally, the chains typically offer extended hours and significant discounts via their hard-to-match advertising budgets.

How will small dental practices meet the challenge? One approach is to avoid trying to match the chains' strengths and take advantage of their weakness.

# Making Dentistry Personal

Corporate dentistry's weakness is that it's impersonal. There's some evidence to suggest that the new graduates who seek corporate employment don't stay all that long. It's hard to build trust with a patient when he or she is seeing several doctors over the course of 18 months.

Corporate dentistry is not the provider of choice for the significant percentage of the population that is looking for a trust-based relationship with a likable dentist and a superior experience in the practice. That segment of the population are patients who will stay, pay, and refer.

Your marketing has to appeal to and attract the dental prospects with the disposable income to be picky about who works on their teeth. Those are the new patients you need to grow your practice in spite of the challenge by corporate dentistry.

## Challenge on Challenge

Corporate dentistry's "playbook" is clear. What's not clear is how your practice will meet the challenges that the rise of the chain presents.

Speaking of challenges, here's another one. We're seeing a sharp rise in direct-to-patient dental marketing from SmileDirectClub—the most prominent advertiser—and other companies. It's clear that this approach cannot and will not eliminate the dentist's role in patient care, but it can cut into the revenue stream of any dentist or orthodontist who offers clear aligners.

The challenges from corporate dentistry don't stop there, unfortunately.

Dental service organizations (DSOs) and DMOs pose a new challenge as they allow groups of practices to centralize services and decrease overhead. Think of it as The Battle of the Economies (of Scale).

Bruce Irick, Comfort Dental's CEO in New Mexico, said in a 2015 article in the *Albuquerque Journal*, "The average dental office overhead is about 70 percent (of monthly revenue). Our overheads are about 45 percent, so these docs are making a lot more money with us."

That low overhead is a *significant* competitive advantage, and it allows the corporate chains and the group practices under management to cut prices and still remain profitable. The small dental practice will struggle to meet those price points.

With large advertising budgets, increased availability, and broad dental insurance acceptance, DMOs can rapidly transform the landscape of a given market. You might think that corporate dentistry wouldn't be interested in your market, and there's a chance that you're right. But if there's money to be made there, corporate practices will arrive. It's just a matter of time.

Finally, the retirement of boomer dentists—who were forced to defer retirement following the Great Recession of 2008-2010—affords both new dentists and the chains more practice opportunities. Many of those dentists have now worked five to seven years longer than they intended to. They're ready, and more than ready, to sell their practices and enjoy life full-time.

But new graduates acquiring existing practices isn't a wash, in terms of competition. Younger dentists are often much more internet-savvy than established dentists, and it's common for the younger doctors to have a correspondingly stronger online presence. They're also likely to have more energy and drive than someone who's looking at retiring in a matter of months.

Basically, they're stronger competitors, and they'll chip away at your new patient base.

And once a chain has acquired an existing practice in your market, you're looking at a completely different level of competition. It's very hard, if not impossible, for a solo dentist using a traditional dental marketing approach to go head-to-head with a corporate practice.

## The Rise of the Groups

While I'm at it, let's not forget that large group dental practices are rapidly increasing in numbers. You can think of those as the midpoint between the small dental office and corporate dentistry, with some advantages of each. More doctors means more availability and potentially a broader range of specialties. And having those dentists in one location means bulk ordering with reduced prices and economies in terms of staff people.

At the same time, patients are more likely to be able to see the same dentist over time. In the rare instance where that dentist isn't available, patients know they're seeing a close colleague.

Large group practices don't have the same trust deficit that the chain practices have. Groups are likely to be able to retain more patients over time.

So keep an eye on any group practices that open in your market. It's possible that they'll be your biggest competition going forward.

This might paint a pretty dark picture, but all is not lost by any means. It looks like help is coming from an unexpected quarter.

# California Strikes Back

Sometimes, serendipity is our friend.

The California Dental Association (CDA) announced on June 27, 2017, that it had formed The Dentists Service Company to help members compete against corporate dentistry and the increasing number of large group practices.

The company features a group purchasing program to help members save money on dental supplies. By report, those savings are enough to level the playing field somewhat and allow small practices to compete more effectively.

Whether this development and other innovations by the CDA will go national is anyone's guess. It's also not clear that, as the competition ramps up even more, group purchasing power will be enough to keep small practices competitive.

So, the corporate chains, the dental service organizations, and the large group practices have been met on the battlefield by a (now) somewhat better-equipped opposing force.

This means war, and for almost all dentists, the battles will be waged for a 70 percent share of any given market. That's a strategic mistake, frankly. Why would you want to engage competitors where they can maximize their strengths?

Hold that thought—it'll be very important to your ultimate practice success.

## Serendipity Strikes Again

About seven months after the California Dental Association announced its groundbreaking steps to support small dental practices, corporate dentistry took another hit.

The Associated Press announced on January 10 that Benevix LLC and its Kool Smiles dental chain had settled a Justice Department lawsuit alleging improper billing practices on Medicaid claims.

According to the article, "Prosecutors accused Benevis and Kool Smiles of performing medically unnecessary procedures on children between January 2009 and December 2011."

The settlement was for $24 million, to be divided among 17 states, three whistleblowers, and the federal government.

This suit is just the latest of numerous instances of corporate dentistry being penalized for providing unnecessary treatment and submitting fraudulent billing.

But that lawsuit isn't the only legal challenge that Kool Smiles is facing. A wrongful death lawsuit was filed in Arizona after the tragic death of two small children following dental treatment.

As these two examples confirm, corporate dentistry has a trust problem. You can and should exploit that weakness by positioning yourself to prospects as **the trusted dental expert**.

If you want to experience ultimate dental practice success, fight the enemy where they're weak, not where they're strong. Because where the corporate chains are strong, they're very strong indeed.

## The Problem of Insufficient Funds

Many people in the U.S. can't afford more than basic preventive dental care, and some can't even afford that. There are two reasons this is true.

Wages for most of the U.S. have been essentially flat since 1973, up just 9.3 percent through 2013. However, prices for dental services have risen **45 percent** just since the year 2000. In dollar terms, the cost of dental care has outstripped the ability to pay for that care by **at least 500 percent**!

And with dental insurance companies shifting more of the payment burden to patients and lowering reimbursement rates, it's no wonder that many people accept only the treatment that insurance will cover.

That's why you get price shoppers, insurance-driven patients, and one-and-dones in your chairs. It's all they can afford. In this scenario, the low price "wins."

"Wins" is in quotes because being the discount dentist is a tough way to make a living. You can stay busy if you cut your margins to the bone, but you won't make the kind of money you want and need. And you'll work yourself and your staff half to death in the process.

Of course, you may well not succeed. As you've seen, low price is where corporate dentistry can and does dominate. Remember—if the chains haven't entered your market yet, they almost certainly will.

Dental practices must grow or perish. It's no longer enough to work to maintain market share … because you won't. And the patients you do get will continue to have low case value for your practice.

The traditional model of the dental practice is eroding, and if you don't take action soon, you may find that the ground is slipping away beneath you.

In fact, the ground that you once considered rock-solid may be eroding.

## Surprise! Your Specialty Practice Is Not Immune

Specialty practices like orthodontics haven't had to worry much about the corporate chains. That situation is changing. It's not just the general dental practice that's at risk; orthodontic and dental implant practices are faced with growing corporate competition as well.

If the business model proves out, be on the lookout for future inroads into other revenue streams. Think professional-strength teeth whitening programs through the mail, press-on temporary veneers, or some version of a snap-in-place smile.

None of those ideas might happen. But remember—if there's money to be made, somebody will figure out one or more ways to make it happen.

Here are some thoughts on the issue from our September 23, 2017, Patient Attraction Podcast™.

# Corporate Dentistry Specialty Clinics Are Targeting Your Revenue

Patient Attraction Episode 1086

Corporate dental practices pose a severe challenge for many general dental practices. With their economies of scale, a general corporate practice can undercut private dental practices on price and generally offer greater availability. There's a growing trend toward one type of specialty corporate dental office that could pose the same challenge for implant practices. After the break, I'll tell you how general dental practices and specialty practices can meet and beat corporate dentistry's threat. Stay tuned.

I'm Colin Receveur, CEO of SmartBox. Thanks for watching the Patient Attraction Podcast™.

If you offer dental implants in your practice, let me ask you a question. Do you think you could compete on price against a specialty corporate dental implant practice?

If you answered yes, how long do you think you could wage a price war against that practice? Unless you have incredibly deep pockets, the answer is almost certainly not long.

You might think that you won't have to worry about specialized corporate dental practices in your market. You're probably wrong about that. To take just one example, ClearChoice Dental Implant Centers have 32 offices and 70 clinicians in their nationwide system. They advertise that they've done more than 40,000 cases. And they offer some version of teeth in one day at a fixed price to their patients.

The writing is on the wall for dentists who are willing to read it. Corporate dentistry is coming after the individual, big-ticket revenue streams of private practices. With corporate dentistry's economies of scale, private practice dentists will struggle to maintain their cash flow from those streams. And that's a hit that not every practice is going to be able to withstand.

If you want to ensure that your dental practice doesn't become another corporate casualty, you need to act now. It's possible to segment dental patients into two broad groups: those who are price-driven and those who aren't.

The price-driven patient is corporate dentistry's target. Their advertising primarily focuses on price and convenience of appointments. In the case of dental implants, that probably would appeal to 80 percent of the market.

That leaves the other 20 percent, and those prospects should be your marketing targets.

Corporate dentistry has one major liability that by its very nature it can't overcome. It can't and doesn't engender patient trust. If that corporate dental implant patient has a problem, he or she isn't guaranteed to see the same doctor. Most likely, the appointment will be with the first available clinician.

The 20 percent of implant patients who aren't motivated by price are strongly motivated by trust. That patient segment has the resources and the willingness to pay more for the right dentist—one they relate to, trust, and regard as a dental expert.

For most dentists, attracting those better patients will require a shift in their marketing focus. Price-driven advertising won't work, so you need to give your 20 percent of prospects reasons to choose you instead of a competitor to solve their dental problems.

You won't accomplish that through postcard campaigns or newspaper ads.

But you can position yourself as the trusted dental expert by using SmartBox's industry-leading Patient Attraction System™. Not only can you get more patients, but you can also get better patients that will position your practice to withstand competitive threats.

Find out what SmartBox's Patient Attraction System™ can do for your practice. Go to PatientAttractionBlueprint.com and schedule your Practice Discovery Session call.

You'll learn how you can double or even triple your practice.

Or, you can wait for corporate dentistry to siphon away your high-value cases.

Join me for our next podcast. Until then, keep moving forward.

## Take Action Now!

Under current conditions—and I should point out that there's no indication whatsoever that things are going to get easier for dentists—both general and specialty practices are at risk. It's very likely that the competitive pressures are only going to intensify as time goes by.

Don't let that time go by without shifting your dental practice to the **ultimate success** footing. It's vital that you act to position your practice—general or specialty—on the high ground.

There is a very specific series of actions you can take to position your practice firmly on solid ground, and we'll begin to look at those steps next. You'll learn how you can not only win the war for your practice's survival but **thrive** like you've never dreamed.

*Whoever admits that he is too busy to improve his methods has acknowledged himself to be at the end of his rope. And that is always the saddest predicament which anyone can get into.*
— J. Ogden Armour

If you know what you're doing, the corporate dentistry marketing machine has an enormous weakness it can never overcome.
— **Dr. Michael Abernathy, Founder, Summit Practice Solutions**

We're different than a lot of these chains, you know. We're a lot more personal, and we cater everything we do towards the patient.
— **Dr. James LoCascio, Highland Township, Michigan**

# "Thrival" Strategies

This book isn't about just surviving, it's about **thriving**—despite the challenges that dental practices face. Here are some handy takeaways from the introduction to keep in mind moving forward.

> **It's true that the traditional dental practice model is dying but not because of dentists' lack of skill or commitment.**

> **It's because of increased competition and decreased insurance reimbursement.**

> **Dentists' advertising traditionally chases price shoppers, insurance-driven patients, and one-and-dones.**

> **Trying to build your practice on those patients is like building a house on sand.**

> **The ground you've built your practice on isn't the only ground available. There's better, more solid ground out there.**

> **Dentists who want to succeed will grab onto the current economic growth trend and ride it for everything it's worth.**

> **You still have time to position your practice for awesome growth and success—if you act now.**

*The dental industry or the dental profession—there are more and more and more and more dentists coming out every year.*

*And there are more and more and more dentists putting off retirement.*

*Competition's going to be more and more and more as time goes on. Who do you want in your corner?*

— Dr. Raleigh Pioch, Salem, Oregon

# CHAPTER 1

# TAKE THE HIGH GROUND: ATTRACTION

*"It's over, Anakin!*
*I have the high ground!"*
~ Obi-Wan Kenobi,
**Star Wars: Episode III Revenge of the Sith**

(Great. But you also have to know how to keep it.)

❝ I've done your traditional things. You know—
I did the full-page ad, and the phone book,
and had a generic website built. I've done a
Valpak mailer for the first several years that
I was in practice, and those things actually
worked—then. But that was 10 years ago,
and then over a two-year period, it totally
dropped off so that I wasn't even recouping
my investment in it. And I realized that a big
change was taking place in how we need to
market dental practices."
— **Dr. Ryan Shepherd, Albuquerque, New Mexico**

I don't usually get biblical, and I'm certainly not compar-
ing myself to the Messiah. But there are a few verses from

the seventh chapter of Matthew that seem very appropriate here. It's the parable of the wise and foolish builders.

> **24** Therefore everyone who hears these words of mine and puts them into practice is like a wise man who built his house on the rock. **25** The rain came down, the streams rose, and the winds blew and beat against that house; yet it did not fall, because it had its foundation on the rock. **26** But everyone who hears these words of mine and does not put them into practice is like a foolish man who built his house on sand. **27** The rain came down, the streams rose, and the winds blew and beat against that house, and it fell with a great crash.

Whether you're building a house or a dental practice, rock is stable ground. Sand is unstable ground.

The ground that's eroding beneath you is sand. As you've read, that sand is composed of price shoppers, insurance-driven prospects, and one-and-dones with little or no loyalty to a dental practice.

The ground is unstable because it's being eaten away by every competitor in your market. Everybody wants a piece of that prospect base. That's not surprising, because roughly 70 percent of any given market is made up of those low case value patients.

But with everybody fishing in the same pool, so to speak, more competitors means a smaller share for nearly all dentists in your market.

You may not know it, but you're in a war for the survival of your practice. If you want to win it, you need to move your practice to higher ground. You see, that prospect base is the lower ground ... but it's not the only ground in your market.

Roughly 30 percent of almost any market is composed of dental prospects who don't care much about low price, specials, discounts, or insurance. The high ground in your market is composed of prospects with **the ability and willingness to pay more** for the right dentist.

The right dentist is someone those better prospects regard as relatable and **the** trusted dental expert to address their concerns. Those prospects, as a rule, are fiercely loyal once they've chosen a dentist. Their lifetime value to your practice is **orders of magnitude** greater than the value of patients in the lower ground.

The high ground in any given market is rock—a stable foundation that you can build your practice on for decades to come.

Just to underscore the benefits of moving to the high ground, here's a Patient Attraction Podcast™ episode from late 2017.

## Are You the "One More Drill and Fill and I'll Scream!" Dentist?

Patient Attraction Episode 1099

Treadmills can be great if you're trying to get in shape or lose weight. But they're a lousy way for dentists to make a living. The dental treadmill is a seemingly endless stream of low-value patients— drill-and-fills, routine exams, and similar unchallenging things. If you've ever gotten to the point where you felt like chucking it all in because you were incredibly bored, stay tuned. I'll be back after the break to tell you how to attract more professionally and financially rewarding patients.

Thanks for watching the Patient Attraction Podcast™. I'm Colin Receveur.

Dentists go through a lot to get qualified to treat patients: four long and very expensive years of dental school, postgrad training, and more. Then there's the expense and the stress of opening and running your own practice.

It seems to me that actually practicing dentistry should be really rewarding to make up for all that sacrifice.

How's the dental profession going for you? Do you wake up eager to face the day and get into the office? Or do you drag yourself into your practice because you know what's waiting for you?

Just another day on the dental treadmill.

Oh, sure, you're doing good work and helping people. So why doesn't that feel like enough?

Could it be because you're not challenged, not doing the cases you love to do? Could it be because your back's beginning to hurt and your neck has twinges? And you've started to wonder just how long you can keep this up?

Or maybe it's just because all your hard work, your physical aches and pains, and your sacrifice isn't growing your practice. You're working too hard, for too long, for too little return and not enjoying it at all.

Yeah, that's discouraging.

I'm not going to cast blame on anybody or anything. You're doing what you've seen everybody else do when it comes to promoting your practice.

It's a simple equation: What you market for is what you get. And how you market is based on your belief about what motivates dental prospects. If you think the best motivators are low prices, insurance acceptance, and discounts, those are the things you advertise.

That's known as the "low-cost strategy," and it's a generic marketing approach that gets generic customers. Or in the case of dentists, that strategy brings in price shoppers, insurance-driven patients, and one-and-dones.

Those low-value patients are pretty much the definition of the dental treadmill. Aren't you and the services you provide worth more than that? Aren't you more valuable than that?

Then act like it, dammit!

The cure for the dental treadmill is to get better patients. Market for the patients you want, not just for what you think you can get.

But you know, not every dentist can do that. What I mean is that not every dentist is *willing* to do that. And even some of the ones who are willing don't have the bandwidth to accomplish it.

Marketing to attract better patients isn't a quick-hit proposition. They're not attracted by discounts and low prices. And frankly, they're not all that easy to convince. They're looking for a dentist they like, relate to, and trust to solve their dental problems. And they start their search for a dentist online.

Google says people consult an average of 10.4 sources of information online before they make a buying decision. If your marketing isn't at least most of those sources, those better patients won't choose you to solve their dental problems. So you need a system in place to get in front of those prospects and stay in front of them, and you have to be where prospects are looking.

That's not just on your website but also on your social media, in your offline advertising, and in your dental emails.

Like I said, most dentists don't have the bandwidth to accomplish all that. SmartBox does, and we do it for more than 550 dentists on three continents to help them get more and better patients.

Are you serious about getting off the dental treadmill and enjoying yourself again? Are you ready to get paid what you're worth?

Then go to smartboxdentalmarketing.com and schedule your Practice Discovery Session™. We reserve these calls for dentists who want to see a Patient Attraction System™ that can double or even triple their practices. You can get more patients, more profits, and more freedom.

And you can get off that treadmill once and for all.

Join me for our next podcast. Until then, keep moving forward.

# Moving to the High Ground

Some of the advertising I've done in the past was more offer-driven, free exam, X-ray kinds of things. When you bring patients in that way, you're chasing them with the next offer or they're chasing you for the next offer, all the way down the line.

— **Dr. James Kiehl, New Hampshire**

Since better dental prospects don't care much about the things you've been advertising your practice on, you'll have to change your marketing approach if you expect to attract them.

As Dr. Kiehl noted, traditional dental advertising chases patients, looking for the "right now" or at least the "soon" decision. The usual approach is to advertise low price, specials, and discounts. But not all offers are equally effective in motivating prospects—particularly if one or more of your competitors are offering a lower price or a better discount.

That "right now" approach leads to the "marketing roller coaster." You'll get good months, a few months with really high new patient numbers, and months with awful new patient numbers.

That's not the best way to run any business, much less a dental practice.

In contrast to the marketing roller coaster, the patient attraction process done right will steadily influence more prospects **over time** to choose you.

That polar shift in your marketing approach is what will move you onto solid ground by attracting better patients with more ability to pay for services. But you're reading this book in part, I believe, because you're interested in **ultimate dental practice success**.

For that, you need to rise even higher. You need a position in your market that's unassailable. Your practice needs to be at the apex.

Reaching the apex of the higher ground requires you to firmly differentiate yourself from your competitors. Why? Because dentists today are **assumed** to be competent until proven otherwise. Unless you ensure that the prospects you want to attract know you're different, and how you're different, you'll be "just another dentist."

Since more than 90 percent of prospects today begin their search for a dentist online, that's where you need to focus your marketing efforts.

> We were at a point where we felt like we got a lot of the portions of running a practice down well. It's just that we wanted to have an opportunity to better market ourselves. We felt like we were incomplete in that area. I wasn't happy with our website. I didn't feel like we were generating the new patients we could from the marketing aspect of things.
> — **Dr. Gregory Stiver, Kansas City, Missouri**

> That's one of the things that I found with my old website was that we did it, and it was great, and it was inexpensive, and two years later, it wasn't anything. It was just there. I didn't realize how much needs to go into a website all the time, and it's just too much for somebody to do who owns a small business.
> — **Dr. Sean Hanson, Salem, Oregon**

# Your Dental Website

Your practice website is the primary information source about you and your practice for prospects. And it's often the first and the last stop for prospects before they call your practice. Dentists who want success need to invest in their websites on an ongoing basis.

Regrettably, that seems to be the exception rather than the rule. Dentists as a group have a "fire-and-forget" mentality when it comes to their websites. I've talked with thousands of dentists, and when it comes to their websites, the attitude is usually like this: "The thing was a pain to get up in the first place, and everybody breathed a sigh of relief when the website was finally done. But we're a busy office, and the website's working well enough. We can't be bothered to keep the website and its content updated."

That's almost a universal attitude. The problem is, that attitude just flat **doesn't work** anymore.

The internet is evolving at light speed, and dentists who don't keep up will be left behind.

Most dental websites look like they were put up 10 years ago. No matter how modern your practice may be, many prospects won't ever see the inside of your office unless your website is also modern in design. Your website is your prospects' **first contact** with your marketing. It's also the **primary** source of information about you, your practice, and the services you offer.

What's the old saying? "You only have one chance to make a first impression." If your dated, outdated, and possibly dysfunctional website doesn't make a good first impression, those prospects are lost to you.

If your website doesn't load quickly and display properly across a multitude of devices, your prospects will click away.

If your website doesn't make it easy for prospects to find the information they want, they'll be gone in a heartbeat.

Content is king as far as Google is concerned. Since Google is still the 800-pound gorilla of search with about a 70 percent market share, your website needs to play by Google's rules. If your content is outdated, you'll take a bad hit in search engine results pages. That equates to **not being found** online, and that's the kiss of death for most practices these days.

If you have dead links, bad links, or spam links on your website, you'll take a hit.

Your website is crucial to actually being found online, and that takes expert search engine optimization (SEO). SEO is an evolved and evolving discipline that takes in a lot of territory, including your site's functionality and ease of use. It's not just keywords anymore.

Unless you have a ton of free time and a talent for SEO, making sure that your site gets seen in local search isn't something you can do yourself. And frankly, it's a huge waste of your time and talents. You didn't go to dental school to become an SEO expert. You spent four long years of study and practice to solve patients' dental problems and get paid well for doing it.

Handling your SEO yourself doesn't directly make you one dollar.

> If you're responsible for your own website, you're never updating or doing the things that need to

be done to stay on top of Google.
— **Dr. Anish Patel, Panama City, Florida**

# Website Content and Tone

Don't make the mistake that too many dentists make with their websites—talking about yourself.

Your prospects don't care how many certifications you have, what postdoc courses you've completed, or what papers you've authored. They don't even care that you might have the best hands in the business. Dentists care about those things. Patients don't.

What's worse, from a marketing perspective, is that a lot of dental websites are written to impress **other dentists** more than to inform prospects. Those sites are often jargon-heavy (without defining terms) and focused on techniques, equipment, and materials.

Your prospects, with very few exceptions, don't care about any of that. They want to feel better, look better, eat comfortably, and smile without embarrassment.

They care that you can **make their lives better**. They care that their concerns will be understood and your practice will take care of them. They care about the relationship they can establish with you and your people.

You'll convince very few people to choose you by talking mostly about yourself, because that's what almost all dental websites do—tout the dentists exclusively.

**News flash: Your website should be less about you and more about your prospects and patients.**

Your website copy—and your social media—need to emphasize **solutions and benefits** at a reading level your prospects will understand. For the internet, a middle school reading level is about right. Just as a side note, writing at that level is a big ask for almost all advance-degreed professionals.

Add in an understanding, caring, and helpful tone, combined with professionalism and specific answers to patients' concerns, and you have the right approach to copy that attracts the patients you want and need to grow your practice.

In September 2017, I sat down with an expert in dental content marketing. Rebekah Carroll is SmartBox's Content Team Supervisor. Here's what she has to say about what makes for compelling content.

# Inside Patient Attraction™ September 2017

**Colin:** The mantra in online marketing is that content is king. Now, not all content is created equal. Google looks at different kinds of content and rates it in different ways. Fresh and unique content is key to getting a top Google ranking as well as attracting more and better patients. In today's Inside Patient Attraction, I want to bring in one of our senior writers and also the manager of our content team to talk about what it takes to attract more new patients in today's Google-centric world. Stick around.

Welcome to Inside Patient Attraction. I'm Colin Receveur, and I'm joined today by the head of our content team, Rebekah Carroll, who we're going to be talking with today about creating unique content, how to leverage content marketing, better search engine rankings, as well as just attracting more and better patients. So, Rebekah, welcome on to the show.

**Rebekah:** Thank you.

**Colin:** You've been here at SmartBox for a long time now.

**Rebekah:** Yes. Yes, I have.

**Colin:** What's kept you here all these years?

**Rebekah:** You know, I really have enjoyed watching the company grow and just being a part of all of that.

**Colin:** You started out really boots on the ground writing the content, and now you're managing our content team of what, 12 people?

**Rebekah:** Yes.

**Colin:** And overseeing all of the content that gets produced, from book writing, to emails, to onsite content, to fresh and unique content across the board for all of our clients.

**Rebekah:** Mm-hmm.

**Colin:** What kind of day-to-day—how do you spend a lot of your days when you're working with our content team to produce that?

**Rebekah:** I do a lot of jumping around from different things. A lot of it is talking to the writers about what they're creating and how to prioritize what they're doing, but also looking at content, making sure that it's hitting the marks that we want it to hit. Then just managing what's coming in and how we can get it done as quickly and efficiently as possible.

**Colin:** When you're working with our content team, what do you tell them about content and SEO? How are those two connected?

**Rebekah:** Well, SEO is imperative in content. The content that we write has to be able to be found on Google; otherwise, it's completely worthless. So we are building in things for SEO keywords, we're building the content in a certain pattern or organization so that when someone reads it, it's effective, and we're trying to make our doctors look like the experts. All of that feeds into the SEO power behind our content.

**Colin:** When you're producing fresh content that's Google-friendly, what kind of different content can you put together?

**Rebekah:** Google likes a lot of different kinds of content. So we write a lot of just blogs. We write a lot of quizzes that are interactive. Infographics that someone could look at and get the information really quickly. We're also highlighting videos and pictures from our doctors' offices. So we're just doing a lot of things that would be interactive, that someone could look at and get information quickly and hopefully make a phone call.

**Colin:** Why does Google like fresh content?

**Rebekah:** It shows authority for the doctor. When Google is looking at that website, it shows that the doctor is paying attention, that they're adding new information, they're staying up-to-date, and that they're actually trying to use their website effectively.

**Colin:** Do you find dentists that haven't updated their website in a while?

**Rebekah:** Absolutely. A lot of dentists like to put that content up there, and then they forget all about it, and then they don't even look at it for years. They may be adding services, or Google may be changing, and they're just not paying any attention to it.

**Colin:** Kind of a fire-and-forget mentality and—

**Rebekah:** Yes.

**Colin:** Then 10 years later, they realize they've got no ranking and no patients coming from their website?

**Rebekah:** Exactly.

**Colin:** When you go into working, when we start working with a new dentist, and they've got a website that hasn't been updated in a decade, what kind of different pieces of content are you working with, and how are you building that out for them?

**Rebekah:** Well, we're going to start by just figuring out what they want to have on their website. Then we're going to build that website the way that they want it. So we're going to focus on those services that are going to get them the patients that they want. So all of our content is going to start there and then branch out. We'll hit everything that they want us to talk about. But we want to focus on their niches and the services that they want to attract.

**Colin:** How do you make a doctor more attractive or more appealing in, say, implants or Invisalign niches?

**Rebekah:** We try to make our doctors be the rock stars.

We say that a lot, actually, that when we're writing, we want the doctor to come across as the rock star. They're the only person on the planet who you would want to perform the procedure that you're looking for. So we talk a lot about how that doctor is special. What makes that doctor the one in their area to perform that procedure.

**Colin:** When you're building this material out to make one of our docs a rock star, how do you compare that doctor to, say, a corporate chain that is their competition?

**Rebekah:** Well, we know a lot of corporate dentists are not giving patients personalized care, and that's what a lot of patients are looking for. So when we're talking about a doctor, we want to make sure that we make it very evident that when someone walks into their office, they're going to be a person, not a number. That they're going to get the care that they're looking for. That the doctor is going to take the time that they need to get them what they want.

**Colin:** What about becoming an expert by writing a book? Do you do a lot of that for our clients?

**Rebekah:** We do. A lot of doctors find that beneficial to have that in their office where they could hand somebody a book about, say, dental implants and say, "I wrote the book about dental implants." It's a great way for a dentist to close a sale, but also it's beneficial for the patient to be able to see what they can expect and what's coming their way.

**Colin:** When you're producing content—you guys produce a boatload of content for our docs—how many pieces on average does it take for a doctor to have a solid search engine ranking? How much fresh and unique content do they need?

**Rebekah:** It really depends on the doctor. It depends on their area and their competition and what they're trying to accomplish in Google, how many new patients they're trying to attract, but we find a range between 2 and 12 pieces per month is about right for most of our clients.

**Colin:** All this content that we're producing for our docs, how do you write it with persuasiveness to get people to call? What kind of tone and grammar do you use?

**Rebekah:** We are working with a team of highly professional writers. We have people who have been writing for decades on our team with master's degrees. They really know how to write in the persuasive method. They know how to organize the content so that what the reader is looking for is prevalent. So as a person reads through our content, the idea is that they would make that phone call after they see the information that they're looking for. Now, we're going to include a really high standard for grammar, spelling conventions to make sure that it's clean, but also we want it to be something that anyone could read. Anybody walking off the street could read it.

**Colin:** Rebekah, what do you normally see when we bring on a new client and the dentist himself or his front staff has written the website copy and has written a lot of that content themselves?

**Rebekah:** Sometimes it's decent, but a lot of times, what we find is that it's just not what Google is looking for.

It's going to be lacking keywords, which means that SEO is weak. It's probably not going to be organized very well. A lot of times, we find grammar and spelling mistakes. Basically, it's just not as strong as it could be, and it just needs to be reworked.

**Colin:** Do you see any issues with how patients perceive the content that dentists write versus what maybe patients are looking for?

**Rebekah:** I think patients are looking to see that the doctor is who they are looking for. A lot of times, the offices aren't able to produce that content. They're a little too close. They need somebody to come in and see them for who they are and express that through their content.

**Colin:** Sometimes they get a little too technical in the weeds, maybe ...

**Rebekah:** Yeah.

**Colin:** ... about accreditations and clinical certifications that maybe patients don't understand what that is ...

**Rebekah:** Right.

**Colin:** ... or what that translates to.

**Rebekah:** Right. Or they might get caught up explaining the nuts and bolts of a procedure when really, the patient just needs to know that this is a procedure for them. Then they can talk about the nuts and bolts in the office.

**Colin:** With our writing team, we've got such a capacity to produce so much great content, but why not take a doctor in Indiana and a doctor in California and use the same content?

**Rebekah:** Well, Google really frowns upon that. We've seen doctors come through our pipeline who have done that and they've just not seen the results that they're looking for. Google is not going to give them the SEO boost that they need to show up in front of patients. So we write all of the content unique so that the doctor has the best chance to be the authority and to show up first in Google.

**Colin:** That's what some doctors may have heard of as a "duplicate content penalty"?

**Rebekah:** Yes. That's it. We see it, and we get very afraid when we see it because it's not good, and we don't allow our writers to do it. They may write about the same topics, but they are not going to write about that same topic in the same way.

**Colin:** If you're not attracting the types of patients you want, if your practice isn't growing, if you don't feel like you're thriving, let us take a look. You may have duplicate content issues. You may not have Google-friendly content. Part of the blueprint that we can put together for you not only shows you what kind of patients and how many of them we can help you attract to grow and thrive, but how things like content and SEO play a major factor into getting the results that you need. Rebekah, thanks for being on the show.

**Rebekah:** Yeah. Thank you.

**Colin:** Pleasure to talk content, talk shop a little bit, and find out how you guys are able to help our dentists attract more and better patients.

**Rebekah:** Yeah. It was a good time.

**Colin:** Awesome. Thanks for tuning in to this episode. As always, keep moving forward.

> [The website's] been really easy for me because I don't have to write it, and that was probably the most infuriating thing, having our own website and somebody asking me for content. Me having to read what somebody else wrote and maybe write, "Oh, that's not right," or "Change this, I don't like that wording," or something like that, is so much easier. To me, it was a blessing that you guys got to do all of that stuff because that is what I loathe.
>
> — **Dr. Nicole Hurcomb, South Bend, Indiana**

So, when you have your website up-to-date in terms of design, functionality, content, and search engine optimization, you're golden, right? Nope. There's something else that has to be on your website if you're going to occupy and hold the high ground.

## Why Should Prospects Take Your Word for It?

The sarcastic idea that *I saw it on the internet, so it must be true* will probably never die.

You telling your prospects how their lives can change is one thing. You have a vested interest in looking great online, and people understand that. But your prospects are looking for confirmation of just how great you are, and that confirmation needs to come from someone other than you and your staff.

To give your prospects what they need to make a decision, you must have other people confirm what you say. That's known as "social proof."

Patient testimonials and reviews provide social proof that you're the right dentist for the prospects you want. Not all testimonials are of equal value to your practice, however. Far too many dentists' websites feature an overwhelming number of "everybody here is wonderful!" testimonials. There's some value to those reviews, and you shouldn't discourage them, but you need something more. You need dental condition-specific "Dr. X changed my life!" testimonials to attract prospects for specific revenue streams.

Do you want more implant cases? Then you'd better have glowing implant patient reviews and testimonials. The same holds true for cosmetic dentistry, clear aligners, and even emergency dentistry. Market for the new patients you **want**.

With a good number of both types of testimonials, your prospects are assured of a superior patient experience and the benefits of choosing you to solve their dental problems.

# 5 Rules for a Winning Dental Website

1. Your website **must** load quickly and accurately across a variety of devices—desktop and laptop computers, tablets, and smartphones. If you don't accomplish this, nothing else matters because those prospects will be **gone**.

2. Your website has to look modern and contain fresh, unique, updated content presented at the right read-

ing level and with an emphasis on the benefits of dental treatment from your practice.

3. Your website has to have superb organization and functionality to help prospects find information quickly and easily.

4. Your website has to provide social proof for your prospects.

5. And your website has to be, and remain, optimized for search.

When your website is visually appealing, provides useful and engaging information, and is easy to use, you're halfway there.

Always remember: Your prospects have more options and more information than ever before. You can't afford to miss a trick when you're trying to attract new patients.

In July 2017, I sat down with David Lange, SmartBox Senior Graphic Designer, to discuss what all is required to design a great user interface (UI) and create an outstanding user experience (UX) that leads to more new patients in chairs.

# Inside Patient Attraction™ July 2017

**Colin:** Welcome to Inside Patient Attraction. I'm Colin Receveur. I'm gonna be joined today by David Lange, who's one of our senior graphic designers, and David is gonna talk to me today about how to get more patients from your website, using great UI/UXs, it's called—the buzzword—user interface and user experience design. Stick around.

Welcome to the show, David.

**David:** Good to be here.

**Colin:** Awesome to have you. Talk a little bit about what engages patients online, and how do you get patients to take action?

**David:** It starts with understanding the user. You wanna understand where they're coming from and what their mindset is and build the site around them, build the features of the website and the content, and make sure it's addressing their needs, and it's compelling to them. If it's addressing their needs and giving them the information, then yeah, absolutely.

**Colin:** You've been doing this for a decade now, designing sites and looking at user interface and what's called user experience, which is trying to figure out what motivates people to take action, what experience they're having on a website. Did I explain that well?

**David:** Yeah. I've done a lot of things, I've had a lot of experience, and I've tried to apply that towards UX design, and yeah, trying to understand the strategy of building a website—not just adding content to the page or filling a page out with a certain amount of words or images or whatever, but really understand what the mindset of the prospect is and how the website design can get them engaged with the practice and the site and all that.

**Colin:** What kind of bad practices have you seen with websites that you see that come in and that doctors have had designed other places? Give me a list of a few of your top pet peeves that you see.

**David:** A lot of times, it's just clutter. It's just very, very dense, very cluttered, unfocused sites, really. There may be a lot of content there, but it's not assembled in a way that drives conversion, which is one of the foundations of good user experience design. Because whatever else your website is, it's a marketing platform, it's a sales tool, and that's what a good UX is designed to do: bring the users in; once you have the qualified potential prospects on the website, you wanna drive them towards conversion and engagement with the practice, so as far as bad practices go, it's everything.

There's some really, really terrible websites out there, and it's usually just clutter and a lack of focus, diluted content and a lack of a clear message. Then there are just some basic things, like the information isn't there that they need, the details and all that. Some just really core thing, but there's a lot of bad design out there. I've seen just about everything.

**Colin:** When you're starting with a practice, and you're laying out the wireframes and the initial design of what that practice's presence is gonna look like, what considerations do you look at, and how do you design where things go and what it looks like?

**David:** It's different from industry to industry. What we do here, again, we consider the patient, we consider their fears and their concerns and their questions and not only what they need and what they want—which are two different things individually—but what's beneficial to the practice, what their market is and their niche audience, and we consider that. Then every component that we put on the site, the information and the header and the navigation and all that, we consider each piece of that to really speak to the needs of the people using the site, to make sure it's clear and concise, the content speaks to their needs, and it represents the practice in a really appealing way, and really sells the brand. It's considering every single component—How is this fitting into that scheme of things, and where does it fit into the conversion funnel? How is it driving conversion?—and answering questions, and always moving forward, always getting that engagement.

**Colin:** In the language of the dentist and their patients, what you're really trying to figure out is what drives this patient to make that decision to choose this practice.

**David:** Exactly.

**Colin:** Would you say that's the distilled singular question that we have to ask ourselves?

**David:** Absolutely. Yeah. We're looking at, Where are they coming from? What are they thinking? And ultimately, point A to point B. Point A ... The buying process can be a very extended process. There's different people at different stages, and we consider all that, but yeah, it's point A to point B. What gets them to engage with the practice? Where are they coming from? What can we put on the website that's really gonna sell the practice and let them know that this is the practice for them, that they wanna engage with?

**Colin:** This engagement that I really wanna focus on in our chat today—prior to that, you've got marketing that happens. You've gotta drive people into the site.

**David:** Yup.

**Colin:** Then after this engagement that you have, you have Follow-Up. When we're looking at the Four Pillars of the Patient Attraction System, you've got your Attraction, your Conversion, and your Follow-Up, and your Tracking. We're really centered on the Conversion aspect of it here at this moment, converting them from finding you into knowing and liking and trusting you, and building a website that's going to have the right calls to action to convert those people into clicks and hits and opt-ins, and interested people, interested patients, is the paramount.

**David:** Yeah. When you're on the website, there's all different stages of the process. Like you said, you have the marketing, and even the SEO that's on the website is gonna drive traffic to that site, it's gonna qualify that traffic, and then once they're on there, yeah, you want the right calls to action in the right places. You want the overall narrative of this site to speak to their needs and to lead them to the pages and the information they need. We have different engagement and attraction features on the website, like the call to action that you mentioned is speaking to specific needs, and it'll get people engaged and interested, and then lead them to engaging with the practice, whether that's through a form or picking up the phone, ideally, right?

**Colin:** Yeah, absolutely.

**David:** We're opting in and getting an e-book or more information and allowing the practice to continue to market to them throughout that discovery process, that buying process, whether they do it once they get on the site, they pick up the phone, or if they leave—they're doing a little more research or whatever—the practice can remain in front of them. That's one of the things we consider, is all the different levels of that process and the different engagement features that can allow the practice to stay in front of them.

**Colin:** Let's talk a little bit, David, about UI and UX and how does that fit into the comprehensive strategy of what we're doing here at SmartBox?

**David:** One of the things that we always look at is the entire journey, the entire buyer process that the prospect is on. We understand that when they get to the website, some people are ready to pick up that phone right away, and for certain services, that's the case. But other people, for more advanced services, they wanna do a little more research, or they have some anxiety, or things like that, and so we understand that not every buyer's in the same position in that journey, and so we kinda try and contextualize it on the site, have the information accessible to people who just need the information, the address, the hours, the phone number, whatever it is, but then understand that a lot of people are gonna click into the site, they're gonna do some research, and then they may come back later, or whatever.

For us, that means putting alternative engagement and attraction features on the site that allow—and I think we mentioned this before—the patient to opt in, to provide their email address, get an e-book, some more information, and really allow the practice to remain in front of them and continue to market to them throughout that decision-making process, so they're always relevant, and they're always in their mind. And so when they come back to the site, or they're ready to make that buying decision, the practice is relevant.

I think Google says that people—I think the number's 10.4 different sources of information that people consult before making a decision, and sometimes that's different and it fluctuates, but the point is, people are making a decision. It's a much more extended process.

**Colin:** They have a lot more information available to them.

**David:** Absolutely. There's different ways that we get information. People are on their phones, and they're coming to websites in different ways, and we try and understand the context of that journey and that mindset and really build the content to kind of understand that and direct that, but also provide opportunities for the practice to continue to market to them and stay relevant.

**Colin:** How do you ... You talk about customizing and enhancing that content to really tailor to that person and where they're coming from, what's going on in the conversation in their head right now—but how does that actually play out? What's that really look like?

**David:** On different pages, it's different. One of the things we try and do here at SmartBox is to really understand the mindset, and we can do that because we work in one industry. On the pages, we take each component and we consider, What is the purpose of this? If it's copy, it's how is it speaking to, and what are they thinking, and what are their concerns at this point, and the questions they have, and all that? We structure the entire information architecture that way, so that it has a flow, and it has a point, and it's speaking to the audience in a way that they can relate to and that's engaging to them. Then it leads them into the calls to action and those different points of potential conversion, and so it's just a strategic approach throughout.

**Colin:** When you're looking at before and after, from what you've done to where the doctors come from, how do you show that what you have done has improved, or do you have case studies? Is this UI/UX thing really just a buzzword?

**David:** Yeah. User experience design, I think it's become more of a buzzword, but it's always important. It's there whether it's good or not. It's not something that we put into the site because we're gonna sell you a buzzword or something like that. It's just the strategy of conversion as much as anything else. You're selling yourself, your brand, and your practice, and when you're doing that, it's harder to sell anything if you don't know who you're selling to. User experience and getting inside the mind of the prospect and understanding where they're coming from, it's easy to understand why that's beneficial.

There have been a lot of studies that show things like changing button text or positioning or placement—where things are and how easy they are to access on a website—can dramatically change the engagement of the user. There's a lot of very subtle things you can do, and it makes a big difference.

**Colin:** One of the really brilliant marketing people that I follow, Dean Jackson, and then Joe Polish, who have a great podcast together and a lot of great information, they talk about entering the conversation that's already happening in the minds of your clients, customers, patients, your people that pay you money and keep you in business. That really sounds like exactly what you're saying. You gotta figure out where they're at and then pair your conversation, your marketing, to fit what they're thinking, to meet them where they're at.

**David:** Yeah. That's a good point. The idea that there is that ongoing conversation, it fits into the idea of the journey. They have concerns, they have things that are going through their mind, and, yeah, you wanna create content that speaks to them. It speaks to their issues and their problems and that niche market. Yeah, that's one of the things you definitely try and do, is kinda get in there and insert your brand as the solution to whatever problem that is, and speak directly to that. That's a good way of looking at it.

**Colin:** Speaking of meeting people where they're at, you're gonna have all kinds of people that visit your website, or my website, or a dentist website. How do you accommodate, because everybody's in a different place—you don't necessarily know where they're at?

**David:** That's sort of the art of the conversion funnel. We know that there are people at the beginning of the awareness stage of, "I just realize I need this service, or I want this service," or whatever. There's people who are just looking for more information. There's people who are shopping by price or different things like that they're really looking for, and then there's people who are ready to commit, ready to buy, so there's people at different stages of that, so there's an art to how we write the copy and how we assemble the pages and making sure that we hit all the points along the way and, again, provide the information that they need, for those people who are ready to buy and really hopefully encourage them to engage with the practice, but then also include those alternative engagement features, so that we're kind of catching everybody at every stage of the process.

The people in the beginning, we wanna be able to allow the practice to market to them, but the people who are ready to purchase, we're there to try and nudge them in the right direction and really sell the practice and the brand and alleviate any last-minute concerns or anything like that, and put them in that position where they're comfortable to commit and pick up the phone. It's a very overview-type strategy, where we try and account for everything in little, subtle ways throughout the copy and the features and the placement of things and all that.

**Colin:** What about for dentists that are watching this here today, and they're thinking, "I built my own website; I can do this"? What would you say to them?

**David:** I've always been an advocate of letting the experts apply their trade. There's things that you can pick up, and there's things that you can learn, but UX design, it's like any of the multiple disciplines that we do here. It's not something that you're gonna be able to effectively apply on your own. Unless you have a lot of time to devote to study and research, it's just not something that you're gonna be effective to do while you're trying to also manage your practice, whereas at SmartBox, we focus on that, and we have all these different departments and disciplines that it's all we do.

Even if you do some research, even if you have a lot of time, there's still the technical aspect too, that you're not always gonna be able to implement changes on your own website. You're gonna be limited in so many different ways. Even if you feel comfortable with user experience design, there's always copywriting and SEO and just all the other dynamics of it, that it's not something that I would advise a hobbyist or an amateur to try and do on their own, for the sake of their practice.

**Colin:** Yeah, I think that's right in line with what we really try to do here as a whole at SmartBox, is keep dentists doing dentistry. The dentist's most profitable activity is doing dentistry. They're tinkering on their website and UI/UX and doing all these other things, they're not doing dentistry. They're not driving their practice. Let the experts handle your training and your staff and your marketing and these other things that we've built out here solely to keep dentists doing dentistry.

For those dentists, as always, that watch our webinars, you know that if you wanna know how your website or how your user experience stacks up against what our best practice is right now, what we're doing to attract and compel and convert these patients into phone calls and butts in the chair, give us a call. The number's on the screen. We'd love to chat with ya and give you a Patient Attraction Blueprint, to show you a comprehensive approach at how you can double or even triple your practice in the next 18 months.

David, thanks for being on the show, man. I appreciate it.

**David:** Thank you. Great to be here.

**Colin:** Awesome information we shared, and look forward to seeing everybody next month. As always, keep moving forward.

A stellar dental website that provides a stellar user experience is about 70 percent of the battle in being found online. The other 30 percent is composed of your blog and your social media presence.

## Social Media for Dentists

You're not selling equipment, technique, or sedation. You're selling trust and a better life thanks to you solving people's dental problems. Basically, you're asking your prospects to relate to and engage with you.

Social media is the ideal platform for dentists to present a mix of the personal and the professional. Social media is designed to facilitate engagement and interaction. It's astonishing how few dentists use it that way.

For dentists, the Big 3 social media platforms are Facebook, Google+, and Twitter.

The different platforms have unique demographics among users. You'll need to tailor your messaging by platform and the demographics you're targeting on each.

There's a temptation among dentists to flood their social media with articles, discussions of dental conditions, and treatments for those conditions. Resist that temptation: social media is about fostering engagement, not providing an ongoing tutorial on dentistry.

Use the 80/20 rule: 80 percent of your posts should be social and personable. Be sure to respond to comments and questions as quickly as possible to build engagement. But just because you're working to foster engagement with your prospects doesn't mean you can't sell to them.

Promoting posts and using paid ads can help you target

specific demographics.

The "rules" for how often to post and how quickly to respond vary by platform.

Regardless of whether you're focusing on an engagement post or a promoted post, using photos and videos in your social media, and on your website, is almost always beneficial. However, stock photos are generally a waste of time and money when you're trying to engage prospects.

By the same token, steer clear of photos and videos that show gruesome dental problems and/or dental surgery. You're used to it; you audience isn't, and most of them will turn away in revulsion.

Those are pretty broad guidelines, so let's hear from an expert about how to use non-stock photos in your marketing.

## Inside Patient Attraction™ January 2018

**Colin:** Every private fee-for-service dentist in the world wants more lifetime value out of their patients. If you can take and get a better kind of patient, that's what every dentist is looking for. On today's Inside Patient Attraction, I want to show you one thing that you can do today to increase the conversion from your website by 35 percent. Stay tuned.

I'm Colin Receveur and welcome to this edition of Inside Patient Attraction. Today, we're joined by Kaylee Everly, who is one of our photographers here at SmartBox and does an awesome job of working with dentists to help them attract more and better patients into their practice. Kaylee, welcome on to the show.

**Kaylee:** It's my pleasure. Thanks for having me.

**Colin:** Awesome. Let's talk a little bit about photography. It's not just photography. Right? It's a proven way that you can increase conversions from your website by 35 percent. Why is that the case?

**Kaylee:** Well, it is pretty incredible how powerful photographs can be. The right kind of photographs can get a dentist a third more patients, which when you think about it is huge.

**Colin:** That's a huge conversion rate. That's a big change from just going from a template cookie-cutter type website to a really customized one that's really built around the dental practice. Kaylee, let's talk a little bit for all the listeners out there today. What kind of photos and what kind of points when they're doing photography on their website do they need to be paying attention to?

**Kaylee:** Well, Colin, the most important point is that the person in the photo is relatable. You want people who look like the people you want to attract. If you're a dentist and you want to attract people in their 40s and 50s who can maybe afford higher cosmetic cases, then that's the people you want in your photos.

**Colin:** It's like Cialdini's principle of liking. People want to be around people that are like themselves. Right?

**Kaylee:** Exactly. If you see someone on a dentist website who looks like you maybe, and they got this big veneer case done, then maybe you'll be more likely to also get that veneer case done. A dentist website is a perfect place for them to feature their proudest work.

Before and after pictures have a place on any dental website. It's kind of your own social proof. But if you can also have that person that got that incredible veneer case that you're so proud of give a great testimonial, and get a good portrait of them, then that speaks louder than stock photography ever could.

**Colin:** When you're working with dentists, are you just pulling out your iPhone and snapping a few pictures, or what's your secret sauce?

**Kaylee:** Well, Colin, it's not as simple as just pulling out your smartphone and snapping a photo. We do use professional photography equipment. We've got a big flash, some very nice lenses, which do help. They do. But when it comes down to it, people make photographs, not cameras. One of the most important things when you're taking a photograph is composition. Here at SmartBox, we shoot for banner images. Essentially, that's the top image on the top of every page, and it's the first impression that anyone is going to have as to—if they click on that veneer page—as to whether you're the dentist that they're going to want to get their veneers with.

**Colin:** I've heard those called hero images. It's the big image right at the top, and it's the call to action. It's what really triggers people to move forward. They see it, they like the call to action, and they click the button.

**Kaylee:** That's the goal. We want to not only showcase a dentist's great work, but also make it incredibly easy for patients to take that next step.

**Colin:** That's really what it comes down to. It's not photography that you want as a dentist. It's butts in the chairs that you want as a dentist. The photography, all the components of the marketing—today we're talking about photography—go into putting more butts in the chairs for dentists. What are some other things that could just make or break your photography as a dentist?

**Kaylee:** Well, distracting backgrounds are huge, and that's something that most dentists probably don't think about because they're in their office around sharp tools, cluttered trays, messy countertops 40 to 80 hours a week for some dentists.

**Colin:** They're used to seeing mess.

**Kaylee:** Exactly. If I'm a nervous patient, then that's just going to completely turn me off from wanting to go to that dentist. I won't take a single photograph without removing all of the clutter and the scary things first.

**Colin:** That's key. You got to make people comfortable and remove the things that trigger these anxieties and fears within people. If you're taking pictures with it, that's giving them that thing that they're afraid of, you're putting it right in front of them.

**Kaylee:** Exactly, and production value is also a big thing. If I'm a prospective patient and I'm looking at a dentist website and it just looks very haphazardly thrown together—there's poorly lit photographs, out-of-focus photos—then I'm going to assume that they're kind of a cheap dentist and I'm not going to get the quality of work that I need.

**Colin:** First impressions are everything. If you have bad photos, why would they think your office is going to be any different?

**Kaylee:** Exactly. Photographs can make all the difference, and you definitely get what you pay for or don't pay for, in some cases. That will affect the type of patients you attract.

**Colin:** Absolutely. Absolutely. Let's pivot a little bit. We've talked a little bit about practice pictures, but how about the technology showcasing what the dentists can do? A lot of dentists have advanced clinical training—they've got lasers and CEREC machines and advanced tech. How do you put the spotlight on that?

**Kaylee:** There are people who love technology and want to go to an office that has the latest and greatest. I would say I'm one of them, especially knowing what I know about the general field now, but most people relate to people, not things. That's where we try to aim more at portraits of happy patients, interaction shots with doctor and staff, the people who can actually relate to and feel something from.

**Colin:** Dentistry is largely a trust-based profession. People want a dentist that they can—I mean I've said it a million times: know, like, and trust. Right? If your photography and your media and presence and presentation of that can foster that knowing and liking and trusting and get that process started, that's the goal. New patients, new butts in the chairs.

**Kaylee:** Exactly. Another important thing is true with office photos. We want to make that person so comfortable by just looking at your website, that they already feel like they've been in your office before they even step foot.

**Colin:** I can't tell you how many doctors I've talked to that have said after we've done the photography and the video, that they have patients come to them and say, "I felt like I knew you after I looked at your website. I felt like I already knew who you were and everything about you." That's the goal. So many doctors—and I think this is a little bit like an '80s and '90s mentality because there was no web—in order to get the first impression from a doctor, the patient literally had to walk into the office. In today's world, the web is that first impression now, and you don't get a second impression. The first impression is the only one you get.

**Kaylee:** You got it. Patients who are looking for a long-term relationship will respond to those types of photos. Patients with some level of anxiety will be more likely to pick up the phone and call.

**Colin:** I think part of what I had just heard you say there, Kaylee, was that you've got dentists that understand the lifetime value of a new patient. Then, you've got dentists that are just looking for the next new patient. Right? There's a big difference between the lifetime value and $100 emergency whatever-my-insurance-covers-can-you-extract-that-tooth.

If you want to attract better patients, you have to upgrade your marketing. If you're a dentist looking to attract 35 percent more new patients from your website, if you're wanting to supercharge your new patient results from all of your marketing that you're doing, check out our industry-leading Patient Attraction System.

We can show you how to craft your message, your photography, and take all the components together to prompt butts in the chairs out the other end and fill up your new patient schedule. Kaylee, awesome to have you on the show. Thanks for putting your experience and insight into this Inside Patient Attraction.

**Kaylee:** No problem. Thanks for having me.

**Colin:** As always, guys, keep moving forward.

# Welcome to the High Ground

When you market your practice on trust and life-changing results, you're appealing to the 30 percent of your market that can and will pay more for the right dentist. Getting them to notice you and find out about you is the first step.

But the decision to pick a dentist is a process more than an event. You've got to find a way to remain top-of-mind with your better prospects while they're deciding to choose you. You've taken the high ground, but now you have to hold it. That's where Conversion comes in, and we'll look at that next.

*Every man who would do anything well, must come to it from a higher ground.*
— **Ralph Waldo Emerson**

(Well said, sir.)

A consistent goal that we have is to continue to have the new patients come in that are high-quality, who are interested in comprehensive dentistry, and really just want something better for themselves and aren't just what we call single-tooth-type situations. They're more of the fine cases that we enjoy doing, so that's always going to be a goal for us as we move forward with a company like SmartBox to help us with that.

— **Dr. Travis Watson, Marietta, Georgia**

You can stay stuck in 1975 and say, this has always worked for me, but the climate has changed. I mean, I've had conversations with Fred Joyal and he talks about the consumer behavior is almost like a whole 'nother creature now. I've had a practice for 12 years, but if you've been doing this for 30 years and you try and do what you did 30 years ago and think that's going to be successful, I think you've got a long road ahead. And when you try to transition out, that young dentist isn't going to find too many appealing things in a declining practice.

— **Dr. David Maloley, Colorado**

# "Thrival" Strategies

Today's prospects overwhelmingly begin
their search for a new dentist online.

If your prospects aren't finding your website,
they'll choose another dentist.

Up-to-date search engine optimization, a strong
social media presence, and helpful content that
meets Google's standards are the minimum
requirements to be seen online.

Images matter. Include subject-appropriate
photography in your posts and testimonial
videos on your website.

Do-it-yourself videos are very hard to get right.
This is one area where dental practices will
do better to outsource.

*Dentistry is all about people and relationships.*

*Colin Receveur and SmartBox know how to attract new patients to your dental office. They are leaders in their field in dentistry.*

*In fact, they are rewriting the way new patient marketing needs to be done!*

— Dr. David Moffet,
www.ultimatepatientexperience.com

# CHAPTER 2

# PLANT YOUR FLAG: CONVERSION

*There are basically two types of people. People who accomplish things, and people who claim to have accomplished things. The first group is less crowded.*

~ Mark Twain

(Amen, brother. Amen.)

"I can say with all confidence that Colin Receveur knows what he's doing to leverage the internet to help dentists attract more and better patients. His systems guide you on how to attract potential patients to your website, what kinds of blogs, videos, content, and pictures to put on your website, and how to keep your name in front of *potential* patients and turn them into *paying* patients."

— Dr. Michael Abernathy, Founder, Summit Practice Solutions

Most dentists work *way* too hard for way too little. It's not that they're not smart. It's that they're digging for their gold in the wrong places!

— Dr. Woody Oakes, President, Excellence in Dentistry, "The Profitable Dentist"

## Guilty Pleasures

I'm almost ashamed to admit it, but I'm a sucker for the television series *Gold Rush*. If you haven't seen it, the show follows several groups of gold miners in various locations, including the Klondike and Colorado.

I'm awed by the sheer grit and determination of these miners, but I can't help but cringe when I see the obvious mistakes they make. One of the worst mistakes is not test-drilling the claim where they propose to mine to make sure gold is actually there. The other mistake is deciding to remove so much "overburden"—worthless soil, basically, often 30 or 40 feet deep—that they risk going broke just **getting** to the gold.

A prospect who opts in to receive further communication from you is the "gold" you want to mine. Not only that, but by opting in, they've indicated that they're reachable. You want to stake your claim firmly on those prospects and go for the gold.

## You Have Their Attention, but You Don't Have Them ... Yet

You've occupied the high ground of better dental prospects. Congratulations! That took courage, perseverance, and a whole lot of hard work. If you revised your website and your social media yourself, you're doubly deserving of congratulations. Hopefully, you continued to make money during all those extra hours of work.

Regardless, your prospects are definitely aware of you now. You've begun the work of positioning yourself as the **only logical choice** to solve their dental problems.

But your competitors are still out there with their practice websites, social media, and possibly even postcard campaigns. It would be naive to think that just because you've attracted prospects' attention, you'll continue to hold their attention until they're ready to choose you.

You need to plant your "flag" firmly in your prospects' consciousness, and the way to do that is through Conversion.

> Our marketing experience has really been hit-or-miss. It's always been internal, and it's always been just word of mouth from our patients. It's been successful over the years, but now we find that the market's changed a little bit with regard to it, and everyone's a little more digital and technologically savvy, and we want to change with that as well.
> — Dr. Jeffrey Tocci, Wellesley, MA

## "You Keep Using That Word. I Do Not Think It Means What You Think It Means."

The word "conversion" means a lot of different things to a lot of people. Trust me, there's nothing religious about my use of the term. When it comes to your prospects, conversion is less a matter of belief than a matter of willingness.

You convert a prospect to a follower (or a lead) when they agree to accept further communications from you. It's another step along your patient funnel, and with all the competition out there, it's a step you can't afford to ignore.

Conversion is a value-for-value exchange. Your prospect agrees to accept further communications, essentially opting in to your marketing. In exchange for their email address, which is valuable to you, you need to provide something of value to them. Your state dental association may limit what you can offer that has monetary value. In some states, that limit is a firm "nothing."

But your offer doesn't have to come with dollar signs. Your prospects are looking for the right dentist, but they're also looking for answers and solutions to their dental problems.

You can provide those answers by offering valuable information—a white paper, a book written by you (or ghostwritten for you), or similar educational material.

If you're targeting specific dental concerns in your marketing, you'll need a white paper, informative article, or book specifically for those concerns—cosmetic dentistry, implants, or gum disease treatment, for instance.

That's your part of the quid pro quo of Conversion: value for value.

## Where the Action Is: Your Website and Social Media

If an exchange is going to occur, there has to be one or more places for that to happen. Your website is the ideal location for your prospects to opt in to your marketing.

Generally, there will be a fairly obvious description of the offer and a clickable link. Some dentists like to explain more about what prospects will be receiving, while other dentists simply let the link take prospects to a form with fillable fields.

At a minimum, you should collect your prospects' names, email addresses, and areas of dental concern.

You can add fields for phone number and city and state, but you'll do well to ensure those additional fields are clearly marked as optional.

Your social media should work to drive prospects to your website, or at least influence them to check out your website, but you can certainly advertise your offers on social media.

In fact, a promoted post or targeted ad on social media with your offer may yield a crop of new email addresses.

# Stack the Deck in Your Favor

Social proof is an excellent means of influencing prospects to like and trust you. That liking and trust are essential to getting prospects to opt in to your communications.

Social proof comes in two types: videos and reviews.

## Videos

> The things that really stuck out to me were the videos on the website being able to convey in different ways. And more than just words, and I think that allows people to understand what it is that we do. They can read about that later, but I think understanding that and getting to know us in the process [is important].
> — **Dr. Scott Watterson, Jackson, Michigan**

The old saying "seeing is believing" still holds true today. Seeing (as in reading a review) is great, but seeing **and** hearing (watching a video) is extremely powerful.

Web pages with video are 53 times more likely to be

viewed than pages without videos.

Your doctor videos and your patient testimonial videos are the most powerful social proof you can provide for your prospects … if they're done well.

Your doctor videos should speak to your prospects' concerns, the solution to those concerns, and the benefits they'll get from receiving treatment at your practice.

Your testimonial videos should include patients talking about the treatment they received for specific conditions and how that treatment changed their lives.

Done poorly, your videos and testimonial videos can actually cost you new patients. That may sound extreme, but bear in mind that every aspect of your marketing reflects on your practice.

If you feature patients who are hard for your prospects to relate to; who have trouble telling a coherent story on camera; or who appear in videos that have poor lighting, bad composition, poor image quality, or audio with dropouts and background noise, you're doing your practice a disservice.

SmartBox has produced tens of thousands of doctor and patient testimonial videos for our clients. We've produced at least a thousand videos for ourselves when you include The Patient Attraction Podcast™.

We know what works and what doesn't on the small screen, whether doctor videos, patient testimonials, or informational programs. So let's hear from Sean Bailey, our Video Team Supervisor, about how dentists can make effective and compelling videos for their practices.

# Inside Patient Attraction™ May 2017

**Colin:** Welcome to Inside Patient Attraction. I'm Colin Receveur, and today I'm super excited to be joined by Sean Bailey, who's our video production manager. Now, Sean isn't just a video production manager. He brings a wealth of experience and knowledge about crafting patient testimonials to use in your marketing to attract more and better patients into your practice.

And at the end, for those of you that stay until the end, I'm going to give you a little tidbit about my new book that's coming out soon. So stick around.

Welcome on to the show, Sean. Great to have you here. Sean Bailey is our video team manager. And video is so critically important these days. You know, websites with video are 53 times more likely to be found on the first page of Google. And I think something like 300 hours of video is uploaded each minute to YouTube, which shows just the huge breadth of how much video actually gets used and uploaded in this day and age, how important it is.

So Sean, why do doctors—why should they care about video? What's it matter to them? Why would they have any interest in doing video and putting it out there on the web in their marketing?

**Sean:** Well, if you think about it, video is a way for your patients to meet you before they even set foot in the door. As a doctor, if you have video on your website that shows your personality, communicates what you're capable of, and basically allows the patient to know that you can handle their particular issue, then you've already set yourself up for success.

**Colin:** You've become the expert in their eyes. You've built that trust level with the patient, from just being the dentist, the commodity, to being the guy that can fix their problem for them.

**Sean:** Exactly. And even better than that, of course, as a doctor, videos of yourself and your abilities are great. Videos from your actual patients are even better. If you have video on your site of patients that have received care from you, successful care from you, and they're able to talk about it clearly, and how it's affected their lives, that's the social proof that you need, really.

**Colin:** I mean, that's one of Cialdini's major weapons of influence, is powers of persuasion—using other people's endorsements to build you up, the doctor, the dentist in this case, as the expert in implants, or whatever niche that dentist wants to be seen as the go-to guy in their market area.

**Sean:** Exactly. So, really, patient testimonials are great, but the right kind of patient testimonials are what you are looking for to promote your service, and your practices. Make sense?

**Colin:** It does. Well, let's hit the counterpoint to that a little bit. What's the wrong kind? What kind of testimonials don't you want?

**Sean:** So, if you pick the right person, someone you like, someone you've offered care to, someone that's happy with your services, that's good, that's a good place to start. But ask yourself: What do you specialize in? What are your niches, more or less? And if those patients don't fit that, they're probably not going to be the best videos to place on your website.

I can tell you, I was on a video shoot, the dentist wanted to ... his feature services were implants and I believe cosmetic cases, like veneers, whitenings, things like that. They brought us orthodontic cases specifically. And they were great testimonials, good people, but did not fit what he was trying to accomplish. So his clientele coming in was probably a lot different than what he was hoping to see.

**Colin:** Kind of hard to be the expert in implants and cosmetics when you're having a bunch of teenagers talk about orthodontics. Another one of Cialdini's weapons of influence: People want to be around people they deem like themselves. It's what I call the mirror effect. You look in the mirror; if your marketing speaks back to you, it's a fit, right? If I look in the mirror and see something I don't like, that's not the right fit—that's the wrong fit, as the marketing or the practice that I'm looking to go to.

**Sean:** Exactly. So if you have those patients that mirror what you were trying to accomplish, that's great. From there, we get more technical. We have the right person, we have the right message, and so the next step is making sure we have the right setup for a successful video shoot with them. You always want to start with sound. Does the room have any sound issues that I need to be addressing, or should I maybe shoot in a different room? It helps to just sit in a room and listen for a few minutes. And ask yourself, Do I hear cars going by? Do I hear noise in the next room? Do I hear air conditioning kicking on?

**Colin:** You're going to hear all that in the videos.

**Sean:** Exactly, yes. And really, that's the next step, is asking if you have the right microphone for the job. You and I have microphones that are close to our mouths. Hopefully our viewers can hear us nice and clear. If our microphone is too far back, or we're using the microphone on the camera, for example, the distance from the subject is going to sound like a cave.

**Colin:** The absolute worst thing I guess I'm hearing you say is the doctor pulls the cell phone out and holds the camera up here and says, 'Hey, tell me about your experience here,' right? Because it's got bad sound, it's got shaky video, there's no lighting, the background's probably sitting in the dental chair itself. But even if you just fix the sound and use a microphone, that just takes it up one big notch, is what I'm hearing you say.

**Sean:** Exactly. You're using a dedicated microphone for recording the audio, and it also helps to lock that camera off, too. And even if it's your cell phone, setting it on a tripod or a stable environment and getting rid of that shaky cam goes a long way to holding a viewer's attention. People in Hollywood try to use the shaky cam, and if it bothers you as a viewer for a Hollywood movie ...

**Colin:** Yeah.

**Sean:** ... How much more does it bother you as a viewer for some doctor with the jitters, you know?

**Colin:** So do you recommend doctors shoot their own patient testimonials?

**Sean:** I recommend doctors find the right patients and equip them with the right message. But when it comes to actually videoing the patients, bring in the professionals to do that. Bring in the people that are going to be aware of the sound in the room, and the people that know how to set up best for that type of scenario, the people that are conscious of your background elements, your mic placement, your lighting placement. Those things that you really don't have time to think about.

**Colin:** Mm-hmm.

**Sean:** That someone else is better equipped to think about.

**Colin:** And, of course, you are able to send your video teams here at SmartBox around the country that are equipped with lights, and microphones, and they have all this experience, not only on the technical aspects of how to shoot the video but also on the storytelling aspects of, How do you craft these powerful patient testimonials that are going to get you new patients?

**Sean:** Exactly. And really, we haven't even talked about the postproduction side of things yet. We've talked about how to find the right people, and how to set up for a successful video shoot, but after that, there's editing to be done. Those YouTube videos you were talking about, any of them that go longer than three minutes, they're probably getting turned off. Exactly. So nobody's going to watch something that goes on too long.

So, for any testimonial, unless you just nailed it, there's going to be some cutting. There's going to be some material that ends up on the cutting-room floor. And someone has to edit that.

**Colin:** And then it has to be, of course, put on the website, it has to be optimized. Because websites with video are 53 times more likely to show up on the first page, but that doesn't mean you just get to drop the video on the website. You have to optimize it, and upload it, and there's a whole process, I assume, that goes into that.

**Sean:** Exactly, yeah. So, I guess the big takeaway is anybody can pull out their phone and shoot a video. But to actually make a video that someone's going to watch, that multiple people are going to watch, and benefit from, that takes more effort than I think some people realize.

**Colin:** How much postproduction editing time ... you know, if you have a three-minute testimonial, how much editing time went into that?

**Sean:** If you think about it, that three-minute testimonial was probably more like an actual 10-minute interview. So, my team would watch through that 10 minutes and find the best segments, the ones that communicate what that practice accomplished for that patient, how that patient's life changed. And sometimes, that's at the beginning of the interview, sometimes it's later. But we find those pieces, arrange them in a way that tells a good story. Once we've arranged the story the way we would like, we would typically color correct it, add some music, that tends to help hold a viewer's attention. And of course, attach some information for the doctor's practice, so they know who to call.

**Colin:** Cool. Cool. There's a whole process, a whole system accompanied with all of this, it sounds like.

**Sean:** Yeah, it's a system that really pays off well when you've got the right patient with the right message, and the right people have arranged that for you, then you've got the story you need to convince that person who has that particular issue in their mouth to come and see you about it.

**Colin:** Video's such a critical part of a dentist's marketing presence, and their online presence. Especially for you guys that are looking for better patients, not just more patients. You've got to become that trusted expert in your market area. You've got to become the dentist that your patients look to as the go-to person, right? You've got to become the one that they know, they like, and they trust.

And to do that, you have to have this incredible social proof—it's Cialdini's principles of persuasion, his weapons of influence. And leveraging patient testimonial videos will allow you to attract more and better patients with your marketing.

I've got a new book coming out, *The Four Horsemen of Dentistry*. It's going to show you everything about video, everything you need to know to defeat corporate dentistry, to grow your private fee-for-service practice, to attract more and better patients, and grow those silos, those niches within your practice, to be big profit centers for you.

Sean, as always, awesome to be around. Thanks for coming on to the show today, hanging out, and sharing your experiences. I know the doctors are going to love it, and I look forward to hearing from everybody out there on what they thought, and input for the next episode.

**Sean:** Thanks, Colin, appreciate you having me.

**Colin:** Awesome.

# Lights, Camera ... Dentistry

As you've seen, producing quality doctor and patient testimonial videos can be quite an undertaking. The one thing I'll say is that it gets easier as you get used to your camera and microphone, your lighting equipment, and your editing software.

While quality videos are crucial for long-term success, producing them is pretty much a waste of your time. Just as with doing your own search engine optimization, shooting and editing your own testimonial videos doesn't make you a dime. You make money by seeing patients and solving their dental problems.

You probably didn't go to dental school to be a filmmaker any more than you majored in SEO. As small business owners, dentists wear a lot of hats. The vast majority will do much better to take off all the various marketing hats—content writing, website design, SEO, video production, and so on—and stick with the field they're experts in.

Speaking of hats you shouldn't wear, managing your online reputation is certainly one of them.

# Online Reviews

Reviews are the new word-of-mouth recommendations. Research shows that people are just as likely to trust independent online reviews as they are to trust recommendations from friends or co-workers.

You have to guard your online reputation diligently. Have a program in place to solicit reviews from every patient you treat, but not when their mouths are still numb from their procedures. You'll also need a policy in place to deal with the inevitable negative online reviews, preferably by taking the conversation offline.

You probably shouldn't be the one who directly manages those activities. That's a duty for one of your staff or for a comprehensive dental marketing firm. Your services in this area should be needed only on rare occasions.

Trent Arkema, SmartBox's Vice President of Marketing, will explain why managing your online reputation requires a dedicated system.

# Inside Patient Attraction™ November 2017

**Colin:** The internet is the largest soapbox ever created. It's where your patients are gonna go to leave their compliments or complaints. If you want to dominate online, you've got to pay attention to your online reputation, because it's the new word-of-mouth advertising. Studies show that patients value the online reviews as much, or more, as they trust word of mouth as well.

On today's episode, I'm gonna be joined by Trent, our VP of Marketing. And we're gonna go through everything you need to know about online reviews and reputation. Stay tuned.

I'm Colin Receveur, and welcome to this edition of Inside Patient Attraction. Now, I'm joined today by SmartBox's VP of Marketing, Trent Arkema. Trent, welcome on the show, man.

**Trent:** Thanks for having me.

**Colin:** Glad to have you here to talk a little bit today about a real hot topic with dentists, reputation management. Tell me everything you know about reputation management.

**Trent:** Yeah, it is a hot topic, especially with dentists, as you mentioned. Over 90 percent of people who search for a dentist start online. And so it's out there, and it's real. Really, third-party information about any dentist can be found online, so it's important to manage that reputation online all the time.

**Colin:** How many patients out of the ... You say 90 percent of all patients go online to search. How many of those are looking at your reviews and your online reputation?

**Trent:** I mean, that's why they're going there, really, to search for a new dentist. That's one of the first things they're gonna look at is your review—not only how many reviews you have but what your star rating is. Your star rating is kind of an insight into what kind of reputation you have. If you have a 4.5, yeah, you're okay. But if you have that five-star rating, then you're really looking good, right?

**Colin:** That's like rock star.

**Trent:** Yeah, and it is. The more and more reviews you have, you can have one or two bad reviews and not have your rating go down that far. But if you only have five or six reviews and you get one one-star rating, well, that drops your average to a 3.8. So when that prospective patient is looking at the star rating, they see 3.8 versus 4.9. Who are they gonna go with, right? So it's really important to get a lot of reviews, so you can handle the one or two negative reviews that do come in.

**Colin:** So what you're saying, Trent, is that the hedge

against bad reviews is really getting a lot of good reviews out there, so that, inevitably, everybody gets a bad review, [but] you're not really hurt by it.

**Trent:** That's right, because if somebody's just looking at the rating and not the actual reviews, they don't have time to say, "Hey, is that really true that they really deserve that 3.8?" And you've just lost a prospect, because they're not going to read the reviews, or they're not going to your website, even, 'cause they just saw the star rating.

**Colin:** With online reviews it only takes a little bit of poison to really contaminate that well.

**Trent:** That's true. I mean, people these days trust online reviews as much, if not more, than word of mouth. So a few bad reviews can leave people with a negative impression just like that.

**Colin:** And what's that mean for the dentist? Every dentist out there's gotten a bad review. What does the dentist do then?

**Trent:** Reviews are not only good for patient prospects and getting prospects to build that trust with potential patients of yours, but [they're] also good for communicating with current patients and have them feel like you're actually listening to them by corresponding and replying to reviews that are left for you. It's also a good way for practices to get feedback on what's working and what's not working in their practice. It's not only about getting patients but also responding to patients that are currently at your practice.

**Colin:** Inevitably, every doctor gets a bad review at some point. What's your recommendation for handling that?

**Trent:** I mean, the best thing to do is to respond to that patient, not online. You can respond to that patient online saying, "Hey, sorry that you had a bad experience. We'd love to talk about this." And take it offline. But don't get into a back-and-forth with a prospective patient or a patient online. Do that offline, but definitely respond to it and acknowledge that something bad happened. Don't try to, maybe, defend it online. Take that conversation offline, but know that you're there for that patient. You wanna hear what their problems or concerns are.

**Colin:** What are the most important review sites out there? Where are patients really looking at when they're trying to find a reputation of a particular dental practice?

**Trent:** I mean, with everything online, Google's king, right? So Google reviews are kinda where it's at. You wanna get those Google reviews, because Google shows those reviews in every kind of ad format, whether it be organic search, whether it be local search pack, whether it be paid advertising. They're starting to show reviews as well.

Google, Facebook, your own website, but out in the internet world, you really wanna hit those Google reviews. They also factor into how Google ranks your site. So the more reviews you have and the better reviews those are, that factors into how high you're gonna be placed in the search results.

**Colin:** Trent, a lot of doctors ... I'm getting the question often. They wanna know, How do reviews and reputation, how does it affect where I rank? Where does it affect my visibility? What do you see with that?

**Trent:** Yeah, it's becoming a bigger and bigger factor in how Google ranks your website. I mean, the more reviews you have and the better those reviews you have, the higher you're gonna rank. I mean, it depends on a number of other factors, but that's definitely a contributing factor and only growing as more and more people rely on reviews to pick a business.

**Colin:** What about capturing these reviews? I mean, there has to be a systematic way to not involve a lot of the staff's time and overhead to get it done. How do you accomplish getting hundreds of reviews and a great ranking in a practice?

**Trent:** Yeah, I mean, you always wanna ask for reviews as the doctor, as the practice, as the front staff. But we always know that's not top of mind for a practice or the front office. And it's also not something that somebody wants to hear after spending an hour and a half in a dentist chair, and their face is half-numb, right? That's not the first thing you're thinking of. So you really do need an automated system, where that system sends out a message, whether that be a text message or email, after that appointment happens, to get that response about their experience. So you really need a system to get the number of reviews you do need in order to get those high rankings within the Google search engine.

**Colin:** And we've got a system that can automate capturing all these reviews, make it seamless for the dentist, not have to take your staff's time at a very competitive price point.

**Trent:** That's correct. Everything's automated. We determine when those messages should be sent out, how they are sent out, whether that's email or via text, and can provide results on how those reviews were managed, what sites they went to, and how many of those reviews that we generated for each practice.

**Colin:** Sounds like a really comprehensive approach.

**Trent:** It is. It's definitely a comprehensive approach that we offer. And it integrates with all the other things that we do from an SEO perspective and paid advertising perspective as well.

**Colin:** Reputation management and reviews are money in the bank for dentists. And for those dentists that are using a vendor that they've been with for more than a couple of years, they're probably not doing the latest, and greatest, and the right things to get those reviews into the right places, that's making the biggest impact with how patients are finding dentists right now.

I mean, the whole point of reviews is to get them seen. If they're not being seen by the biggest audience, give us a call. We'd love to show you how we can help you attract more and better patients with our reputation management and our patient attraction systems. Trent, it's been awesome to have you on the show, man.

**Trent:** It was great being here, thanks again.

**Colin:** Thank you, and as always, keep moving forward.

## Conversion Is a Major Step Toward Becoming Your Patient

The decision to choose a dentist is a process leading to an event. When a dental prospect converts to a lead, you have the opportunity to help move them further down your patient funnel. To accomplish that, you'll need a steady stream of content specifically related to their dental concerns and released at the right intervals.

The next phase, Follow-Up, is where leads are converted to new patients. We'll look at that in the next chapter.

> *To convert somebody, go*
> *and take them by the hand*
> *and guide them.*
> — Thomas Aquinas

What I'm most looking forward to out of this process is to help us identify candidates. We know that we offer a service—with the All-on-4® and some of the implant surgery, some of the things we do here—that really isn't available except in some of the larger metropolitan areas, and they're two to three hours away. So, we're able to offer it right here in Bloomington-Normal, in central Illinois, and we'd like to reach out to more people in the area.

> — **Dr. Robert Wolf, Bloomington, Illinois**

A lot of these patients' questions will be answered prior to them coming in, and I know that's what Colin has said, "Let's screen them before they come to the practice, so they know that they're going to the right office," and that's what I'm hoping to see, and just an explosion of new patients that want our services.

> — **Dr. Patricia Takacs, Lexington, Kentucky**

## "Thrival" Strategies

Dental patient decision-making is a process. You need to give prospects the information and time to choose you.

Conversion happens most often on your dental website. Make it easy for prospects to convert.

Conversion is an exchange of value—your prospects' email addresses in exchange for a white paper, article, or e-book.

Market for what you WANT. If you want implant cases, offer something related to implants.

Keep a close eye on your state regulations before offering anything of financial value.

***With your design and your videos
and the way you approach it,
I'm the first person they see when
they're searching in my area.***

***That's my goal.***

— Dr. Kerry Johnson,
Landisville, Pennsylvania

# CHAPTER 3

# PATROL YOUR TERRITORY: FOLLOW-UP

*All adventures, especially into
new territory, are scary.*
~ Sally Ride

(When you're right, you're right.)

**"**The other thing is the drip marketing, and there have been so many times when I think, 'Oh, we should do this and follow it up with that, and then one more thing after that,' and that's a nightmare for me to try to figure out. I'm too busy doing other things and need to be doing other things, and so the way that SmartBox is offering that and able to build a website around those types of things. Very, very important."
— **Dr. Scott Watterson, Jackson, Michigan**

There's an old adage that says, "Don't put all your eggs in one basket." Not everyone agrees. The famed American industrialist, Andrew Carnegie, is credited with saying: **"The way to become rich is to put all your eggs in one**

**basket and then watch that basket."**

Okay, your qualified leads aren't exactly eggs, but there are some similarities. The decision process is a transformative process, much like an egg hatching. Eggs take awhile to hatch, and leads take awhile to make a decision. Both eggs and leads need "incubation" if they're going to realize their full potential, whether that potential is to grace your breakfast table or your practice's bottom line.

Watch that basket, and give it all the warmth it needs.

# Keeping in Touch

Google reports that people consult an average of 10.4 online sources of information before making a buying decision. If you're going to convert leads into appointed patients, you **must** be most, if not all, of those 10.4 information sources.

Fortunately, once your prospects convert to leads by giving you their email addresses, you've got an "in." You convert leads to appointed patients by "dripping" information to your leads at carefully timed intervals.

Timing is crucial. Contact them too often, and you're perceived as being pushy. Contact them too seldom, and you open the door to your competitors stealing your leads.

"Drip" marketing can be a real time suck, as they say. But it doesn't have to be.

# It Ain't Easy Being Right

Drip marketing requires you to send the right emails to the right prospects at the right times. That sounds easy, but it's not. You're dealing with separate content streams for each condition you want to address: implants, gingivitis/periodontitis, cosmetic dentistry, and so on.

Your individual content streams should be designed to take your prospects on a journey from maybe to yes. That's how you get more new patients.

But your prospects enter your patient funnel at different times and with different concerns. It makes no sense to send the sixth email in a content stream to someone who's just agreed to receive communications from you. Every prospect should receive the correct content emails in order for your drip marketing to be maximally effective.

Using a spreadsheet to manually ensure that the right emails go to the right prospects at the right time can eat up a huge amount of staff time.

And there's great potential for error, like sending an email on dentures to a 20-something who's interested in teeth whitening.

Still, some dentists manage to do a credible job of following up with their leads. Some, but by no means all, or even most. Before you go down the road of manual email marketing programs, there's one vital question you need to ask.

## Do You Have the Bandwidth?

If you're fortunate enough to have three or four hundred qualified leads, you're facing a potential logistical nightmare. Let's say that the dates of opting in to your marketing are scattered over a period of three months. That would represent roughly one to two new leads every single day. More likely, you'd have some clusters of new leads on individual days mixed in.

If you have as few as five email content streams, each stream contains patients who opted in (for simplicity's sake) three months ago, six weeks ago, one month ago, two weeks ago, and yesterday. Realistically, you'd probably have at least one new lead on 70 percent of the days in those three months—63 different entry dates.

Somebody—hopefully not you—will have to track each and every lead in your funnel and ensure that the right email in each content stream is delivered to the right recipient at precisely the right time.

Talk about a time suck! But that's not the only time commitment involved in turning leads into appointed patients.

# Producing Email Marketing Content

Before any drip marketing takes place, you or someone you employ has to create the various content streams. That's somewhere between 10 and 15 separate emails for every dental problem you want to address, and an additional one concerning various aspects of your practice.

That's a **lot** of writing, and it's beyond the capabilities of most practicing dentists.

Not only is the sheer amount of writing daunting, but writing effective emails that your prospects will want to read requires a particular skill set.

Your prospects aren't dentists. They won't understand dental jargon. They won't care about techniques or how cool your technology is. And the vast majority of them probably won't have your reading comprehension level.

If you have the time and the ability to write at a 9th-grade comprehension level (recommended for online writing); if you can put fairly complex dental terms into language that your prospects will understand and relate to; and if you can structure each email in each stream to take your prospects on a journey to yes, then you should write your own drip marketing content.

Otherwise, forget it. Hire a reputable dental marketing firm with extensive experience in drip marketing.

## Testing Your Emails for Success

It's a simple fact that some emails will be more successful in influencing prospects to book an appointment. But **which ones**? The only way to know for sure is to test various emails against other emails.

Simple. Not.

An email has many elements: subject line, greeting, graphics, text, copy, call to action (CTA), link, and so on. For your drip emails, you'll have a **minimum** of 8-10 subject lines alone. You should have differently phrased calls to action. You should have different graphics.

The number of possible combinations is mind-boggling, and the prospect of trying to create and then track the results of all those combinations is overwhelming.

Even testing one element at a time—for instance, testing one subject line against another to see which influences people to open the email—is very labor-intensive.

And frankly, if you're creating content streams, sending out emails, and testing various combinations, it doesn't make your practice a dime. You make money seeing patients and solving their dental problems.

Are you ready to give up on the whole thing? You don't have to.

## Don't Capitulate ... Automate!

Email automation is the answer to staying in front of prospects and moving them down your patient funnel. Once a person's email address is added, and that address is placed into the right content stream, the system will automatically select the correct email, add the correct email address, and release the email on the correct day as measured from the date of entry into your patient funnel.

A wide variety of email automation programs are available. Those programs vary in cost, learning curve, features, flexibility, analytical capabilities, and ease of use. Any dentist who's considering automating his or her email marketing should do thorough research before purchasing an automation program.

Just ask Dr. James Kiehl of southern New Hampshire. "I've tried some Infusionsoft marketing on my own," he told us, "and found it very difficult to put all that together. When I saw what SmartBox was doing, I was really blown away by it. You had that solution right there that I could just tap into."

(Full disclosure—SmartBox uses Infusionsoft® and other email automation programs for our dentists.)

Email automation helps to ensure that every prospect in your funnel gets the right email at the right time. But beyond that, automation makes it possible for your dental practice to track the open and click-through rates of your emails without spending enormous amounts of staff time.

You can easily mix and match subject lines, salutations, copy tone and length, graphics, calls to action, and even the design of links to determine which emails are most effective for which patients with which problems.

As noted, email automation programs vary widely, and you'll want to shop around for the right one for your practice. There's no point in spending big bucks for a program that does far more than what your practice needs, or one that takes a year to learn to use well.

## Bringing It Together

Once you have your content streams, your email automation software, a plan to test the effectiveness of your email marketing, and a designated staff member to oversee the results, you're set. You'll be able to meet every new prospect who opts in right where they're at—the beginning of your patient funnel.

Your drip marketing will help those prospects move from lead to appointed patient, and you'll have more new patients in your chairs.

But—getting all that set up is a lot of work, and there are a lot of dental practices that don't have the capacity.

For most dentists, who don't necessarily want to handle another staff person to oversee their marketing, outsourcing to a reputable, dedicated dental marketing firm is the answer.

If you're going to choose a vendor, make sure they have an email automation expert on staff. Someone like Cindy Morus, a SmartBox Automation Specialist. You could say that Cindy has devoted much of her life to making things easier for people.

Here's what she had to say during the February 2017 episode of SmartBox's Inside Patient Attraction™ webinar series.

# Inside Patient Attraction™ February 2017

**Colin:** Welcome to Inside Patient Attraction. I'm Colin Receveur, and on today's episode I want to talk about automation. I hear all these dentists, they're talking about automation, they're talking about, "How do I automate things and make these emails go out? What is this Infusionsoft, Confusionsoft thing?"

Today I'm going to be joined by Cindy Morus, who's one of our automation experts here at SmartBox. I want to show you some real-life implementable examples of what you can do right now to build this automation, how to do it, what to do, and then what the real-life results are from a doctor that put our Patient Attraction System™ to work inside his practice to help him attract more and better patients.

Welcome to the show, Cindy.

**Cindy:** Hey, Colin, thanks for having me.

**Colin:** Appreciate you being here. You've got a cute little saying that you use when you're talking about automating things. Tell me what that is.

**Cindy:** I say, "No more boring, tedious, or annoying. Automate it."

**Colin:** No more sending out one-off emails, and no more spreadsheets, and tracking things? If it can be kept track of, it can be automated, in a sense, that you don't have to touch it anymore.

**Cindy:** That's right, and those are kind of cues to people when they start to feel that. That they can say to me, "Hey, what are we going to do about this? How can we automate it?"

**Colin:** Cool, cool. Tell me about—you can do simple stuff, you can do complex stuff; tell me about the range of things that you can automate within Infusionsoft.

**Cindy:** Yeah, so, by the way, Infusionsoft isn't the only tool we use for automation. There's also Active Campaign, another tool that we use. There's a lot of them out there, different costs, different abilities. These are the two that we've chosen to use with our doctors.

**Colin:** Pretty cool.

**Cindy:** The most common thing that you'll see is where you have a little box on the website, where somebody will give you their first name and email address. That gets them into your system, and you have permission to send them automated emails. Then you can—what we do is we have a series of emails, educational emails that go out to the patients on a weekly basis, educating them about the doctor's services, and getting a comfortable relationship going with the dentist before they might ever come in.

**Colin:** How often are you sending out these emails once you get them into the system? How often are you contacting patients?

**Cindy:** Generally on a weekly basis.

**Colin:** For months, forever?

**Cindy:** Oh, it depends. The doctor approves how many go out. We have some material that they can look at and make some changes, and approve it. Some of the autoresponder sequences are 10 emails, some of them are close to 20. It depends on how much it takes to tell the story.

**Colin:** To get the patient to know, like, and trust you.

**Cindy:** That's right.

**Colin:** That's really what it comes down to, is know, like, and trust.

**Cindy:** That's right.

**Colin:** How do you know that it's working?

**Cindy:** Well, of course we track everything here for our dentists, and we track how many people come to the website, how many people sign up, how long they stay before they unsubscribe, when they actually call into the office, how many people are opening them and clicking on different things. We can track all of that.

**Colin:** Very cool. Tell me about—how do you create these automated sequences, Cindy? What goes into putting them together, and making them work for the dentist?

**Cindy:** Oh, that's a good question. First we start with creating the icon in our program, whether it's Infusionsoft or Active Campaign; that is the box that they fill in. There's code on that that I give to our web development team, and they put it on to the website, and they make it look all pretty.

Then after that, there's a thank you page that they go to. For most of the autoresponder sequences, we send them to another form where they can fill in if they would like to receive a printed copy of the special report. Then there's a thank you page for that. Then after that, they've entered into the automation, and they start to get the emails.

They'll get the first email, and then we put a timer in to make it wait seven days until the next email goes out. We do that all the way through to the end.

**Colin:** They just get one a week until the end of time?

**Cindy:** That's right, and it's totally hands off. We notify the dentist office when someone signs up for, just puts in their email. Then we also send them the special report, and the mailing address if the person wants to get a copy of it.

**Colin:** Then what about creating all these reports, and emails, and content? Who does that?

**Cindy:** Oh yeah, that's a big job. Fortunately I don't do that. I just take what they give me. We do have a department that handles all of our writing. Then they give it to me, and then I customize it and make sure that it's exactly what the doctors approved. Then it's totally hands off, there's nothing that needs to be done.

They can sign up ... You know, people are searching day and night. I actually went through this recently myself, and since we do dental marketing, I tested them. I called several, and one sent me an email about a week later and said, "Are you a patient?" I said, "No."

**Colin:** A week later?

**Cindy:** Yes.

**Colin:** Oh, wow.

**Cindy:** A whole week.

**Colin:** Well, you were gone by then.

**Cindy:** Well, I had chosen someone else, obviously.

**Colin:** Yeah.

**Cindy:** I called a couple more, sent a couple emails, I just wanted to see, do a little market research out in Sacramento and see what would happen. Someone got back to me very quickly, and turned out actually to be a very close dentist. I really enjoyed going. It worked out to my benefit, but I did kind of monitor what they were doing. It wasn't what we do with dentists, what our dentists do.

**Colin:** What you found was that the majority of these dentists that you reached out to didn't even try to contact you back within any reasonable urgency or amount of time?

**Cindy:** No.

**Colin:** I mean, that's something that I know at least on previous podcasts we've talked about, with returning phone calls. New patients don't leave voicemails, new patients aren't going to send you an email and wait around for a week. You've got to have an automated system in place to handle this.

**Cindy:** Right.

**Colin:** So that you're not losing these new patients. I mean, that's just ...

**Cindy:** Right, and they didn't even bother to look and see if I was a patient, or call me. I left them all the bread crumbs so that they could get in touch with me.

**Colin:** It's just laziness.

**Cindy:** Yeah, or lack of systems, lack of automation.

**Colin:** Sure, sure. You know, you've done so many of these. Is there one doctor that really stands out in your mind as like a flagship of somebody that we can talk about, that these doctors that are watching the webinar today can go out and check out, or really see hands-on what this is all about?

**Cindy:** I would have them go look at Dr. Feder's site, he's in Illinois.

**Colin:** Tom Feder in Illinois.

**Cindy:** Right, he had 50 to 60 patients a month coming in before he started working with us, and now he's at 70 to even over 100 new patients a month.

**Colin:** He had a 22 to 1 ROI with us, 2,200 percent return on investment.

**Cindy:** Yeah, take that to the bank.

**Colin:** Take it all the way to the bank.

**Cindy:** Right, and of course it's all automated. He's not having to go out there and produce the content, he's not having to go out and send out the emails—it's all happening while he's still working, or he's asleep, or he's with his family.

**Colin:** All part of the Patient Attraction System™.

**Cindy:** That's right.

**Colin:** What are these campaigns based on? What are you targeting? Why does somebody want to get these emails from you?

**Cindy:** Well, if they're searching on the internet, they're looking for information. There's a lot of information out there, of course, and they're probably finding some of it. This way, the way that we write it is not only educational, but it's really caring. It shows that we're interested in them, and it helps them to get to know us. We know going to the dentist isn't high on people's list of fun things to do, or their bucket list.

**Colin:** I don't think it's on the list at all, yeah.

**Cindy:** Some people are afraid, and have had bad experiences. We try to deal with the things that we know that patients are uncomfortable about, or that they just don't know, and give them really good, caring information.

**Colin:** These areas that we're trying to educate them on, we're talking about the niches in industry. The patient's looking for something specific. Maybe it's sedation, or maybe it's implants, or maybe it's orthodontics, or maybe it's Invisalign, or whatever it could be.

**Cindy:** That's right. We're even working on some now with sleep apnea.

**Colin:** We have that new sleep apnea survey that we've rolled out.

**Cindy:** That's right, it's a quiz. It asks, I don't know, eight or 10 questions, and the people score themselves one, two, or three. Then it actually calculates their risk factor for sleep apnea. Our goal in that particular sequence is, first of all, they get sorted when they come into the automation, so they get different emails. Again, we're segmenting the list, we're targeting and talking to the people. If you're low risk, then we're not going to, we're going to give you different information than if you're high risk.

Our goal for that is to have them come in for a consult so we can work with them on it, because we know how dangerous sleep apnea is.

**Colin:** Yeah.

**Cindy:** We're sharing that in the emails. That we know about it, we care about it, and we know that if you have it, you're miserable, your family's miserable, and your health is in danger.

**Colin:** Yeah. For anybody that's watching this webinar here, for tonight and tonight only, whether you're a current client, a past client, or not even yet a client, I want to make a very special offer to you, that if you want to see what one of these Patient Attraction Systems™ that we've built, like the kind we use for Dr. Feder, and all these different dentists that are killing it right now in their market areas, I want to offer a 50 percent off promo to let you kind of dabble your toe in the water and see what it's all about. Shoot me a personal email; my email address is colin@smartboxwebmarketing.com.

Shoot me an email, I'll send you back the link to the special order form where you can get this 50 percent, $2,000 off order form to get a customized Patient Attraction System™ built for your practice.

Thanks for being here, Cindy. I appreciate you being on the show.

**Cindy:** Thanks, Colin.

**Colin:** Coming all the way from Sacramento to visit us, and talk about how we can help doctors to attract more and better patients. Appreciate everybody here watching tonight. Keep moving forward.

## Once You've Got It Together, Keep It Together

Drip marketing is an important aspect of marketing your practice, but it's hardly the only marketing vehicle. If you're going to get all the new patients you can, you need to know which parts of your marketing are performing and which aren't.

The best way to monitor your marketing's effectiveness, and your return on investment, is through phone tracking. We'll look at that next.

*I'm pretty sure people are going to start writing letters again once the email fad passes.*
— **Willie Geist, Journalist**

(A swing and a miss, Mr. Geist, but thanks for playing.)

"I've been a client of Colin Receveur since 2013. I already had a prominent web presence. Colin and his brilliant team were quickly able to consolidate and automate our online programs—email responses, phone tracking and recording, press releases, blog posts, Infusionsoft integration with ortho and implant campaign sequences."
— **Dr. Mitchel Friedman, Lincroft, New Jersey**

"We need help, dentists, need help with our marketing, we need expert advice. It's, 'I don't want to reinvent the wheel,' and figure out things the hard way. I want somebody who understands things from the patients' point of view and can funnel and get the patients the information that they want—not what I want to give them, because I've done it that way."

— **Dr. Raleigh Pioch, Salem, Oregon**

# "Thrival" Strategies

You have to stay in front of converted prospects until they're ready to choose you to solve their dental problems.

Drip marketing is the ideal method for staying top of mind with prospects.

Automate the email process to get the right email to the right prospect at the right time.

Choose the email automation that you and/or your staff can learn and will use.

Use the tracking features in the program to test various combinations of email elements for effectiveness.

Creating condition-specific email information streams is an enormous time suck. Outsource it.

*One of the features of the SmartBox services that I really like is the drip marketing.*

*As I talked about before, marketing is all about layers and just exposure because patients buy what they know, what they see. If they're not seeing you, you don't exist.*

*You want to build up your business by referrals? Wonderful, continue to do that, but as time goes on, as you age with your patients and your referral bases, those patients are going to get older and older; you're going to need fresh, young patients.*

*Why not do that with internet marketing, obviously utilizing SmartBox?*

— Dr. Raleigh Pioch, Salem, Oregon

# CHAPTER 4

# INTELLIGENCE GATHERING: TRACKING

*You may have to fight a battle*
*more than once to win it.*

~ **Margaret Thatcher**

(According to the 20th-century's longest-serving
British prime minister, no less.)

> **"**One of the great products that Colin has is
> a way to track those by assigning different
> phone numbers to each one of those, and then
> providing analytical data on a very timely ba-
> sis so you can decide if you want to continue
> with a certain marketing effort—is it paying
> off, is it doing well, or do you need to take
> that money and put it in another place?"
> — **Dr. Michael Abernathy, Founder,**
> **Summit Practice Solutions**

We've arrived more or less where we started. If you take
and hold the high ground, convert prospects to leads,
and then nurture those leads, you'll have more and better new patients.

You'll be busy and hopefully you'll be making a lot more money. But before you determine the battle is won, consider this quote from Thomas Edison:

> Being busy does not always mean real work. The object of all work is production or accomplishment and to either of these ends there must be forethought, system, planning, intelligence, and honest purpose, as well as perspiration. Seeming to do is not doing.

Whatever you think about the Wizard of Menlo Park, it's undeniable that the man was incredibly industrious. But—and this is important—he was busy with a purpose. All his activities were directed at achieving specific goals. He was doing research, so he wandered down a lot of blind alleys. In the process, he learned why many things didn't work and **why** a few things did.

Those few things that worked were enough to cement Edison's place in history.

If you're busy, you need to know **why** that's happening. Which parts of your marketing are working and which aren't? Without that information, you can spend yourself broke getting new patients. With good operational intelligence, you can achieve maximum return on investment … and that's good for your bottom line and for your practice's longevity.

## This Isn't a Battle—It's a War

It's a fair statement that the dental practice landscape is changing more rapidly than at any other time in U.S. history. What that means for you is that marketing your dental practice is an ongoing challenge.

I mentioned in the beginning that you're in a war for

your practice's survival. Wars are seldom won on the basis of one or two battles. And the strategy that secures early victories will certainly have to be adjusted to keep winning. You need actionable intelligence about your marketing to accomplish that adjustment, and the best way to get that is **not** by asking new patients.

# Those Unreliable New Patients

It's common for dental practices to ask new patients how they found the practice. That question may be posed when the patient calls for an appointment, at check-in, or after they've received services. It's a common practice, but not an accurate one.

Research has shown that new patients' memories are spotty at best when it comes to recalling the specifics of dental marketing. That's not true in all cases, certainly, but the fact is that you don't know which self-reports are accurate and which aren't. That leaves you guessing about which emails, which print ads, which online ads, or what aspects of your website work to get you the most new patients.

Don't get me wrong—it's great that they found your practice. But guesswork is no way to run a business. You'll risk wasting huge chunks of your practice marketing budget by funding marketing that simply isn't delivering for you. And few dental practices these days can afford to waste money.

## Track Your Marketing Investments

The single best way to accurately track your marketing's effectiveness is through phone tracking. The reason phone tracking is so accurate is that the overwhelming majority of prospects still use the phone to book appointments.

Phone tracking assigns unique phone numbers to different aspects of your marketing. Those numbers automatically forward to your practice phones, and the source of the calls (and often, the calls themselves) are recorded in a database. Depending on the phone tracking package you choose, all calls may be recorded or just new patient calls.

With phone tracking, you know exactly which parts of your marketing prospects are referencing before they call your practice. When you know exactly what's working and what's not to put more new patient butts in your chairs, you can fine-tune your marketing for maximum effectiveness and maximum return on investment.

But phone tracking, done right, will tell you much more on which parts of your marketing are working best.

## There's Many a Slip Between the Ad and the Appointment

Every prospect who calls your practice and isn't appointed is a complete waste of your marketing investment. That's a harsh statement, maybe, but it's true.

You potentially spend hundreds of dollars on marketing to attract a single new patient. When that prospect calls your office, your marketing has done its job. But there's one more step to actually make your investment pay off, and that's to put that new patient's butt in one of your chairs.

Things can and do go wrong at the point of first contact with your practice. When something goes wrong, you're not only out the money you spent to get the phone ringing, but you also lose the money you would have made treating that patient.

Dentists uniformly swear that their front offices do a great job appointing new patients. SmartBox's carefully acquired data strongly indicates that isn't always true. In fact, when we analyzed the data from an entire quarter—from all our dentists at one package level—the results were staggering, and not in a good way.

This wasn't a particularly small sample of dentists, and the practices were located all over the country. What we found was that, on average, between **54 and 77 phone calls to the practice during business hours weren't answered**!

If you take an average case value of $1,500 and assume that 20 percent of those calls were from new patients, those dentists were losing **tens of thousands of dollars a month in revenue**.

You might not believe that's happening with your practice, and you may well be right. **But how would you know?**

Dentists should be spending their time in the operatories solving patients' dental problems, not hanging out in the front office listening to phone calls. True, you might have incidental exposure to some new patient calls, but there's no guarantee that what you hear is representative of your staff's overall performance.

And while some practices require front office staff to track the outcome of their new patient calls, there's no guarantee that the results they report are accurate ... particularly if their raises or bonuses depend on their performance.

Look, I'm not dissing any doctor's front office. I know from experience that the vast majority are honest and very hardworking. That doesn't mean they're doing their jobs as well as they could be. Very few people have any formal training in converting hesitant prospects into appointed patients.

Let's assume your staff is reporting outcome accurately. There are any number of reasons you're not getting all the new patients you could be.

Face it—front offices can be very busy places. If you have dedicated phone answerers, they may also be dealing with patients in the practice, rummaging through files, trying to field multiple calls, or helping calm hysterical children. That's a recipe for unanswered calls and hang-ups. And there's no guarantee that a prospect who calls your practice and hangs up will ever call back.

As you've seen, SmartBox's data shows that a **huge** number of calls to dental offices are never answered during business hours. But again, you won't necessarily know that ... unless you implement phone tracking.

## The Call's the Thing

SmartBox was able to compile that data on our dentists' phone calls for one simple reason—we record every incoming call to a dentist's practice and record the source of the call.

Our Zetetics® Phone Tracking service assigns unique phone numbers to different aspects of your marketing.

When a prospect calls your practice, that call and the source of the call are automatically recorded and saved in an easy-to-access database. That makes it simple to identify which marketing vehicles are generating the maximum return on investment in terms of new patients in your chairs.

But we don't stop at accurately tracking your marketing ROI. Our dedicated team of Call Quality Analysts listens to every phone call to every practice. That allows us to identify problems with a dentist's front office staff technique in appointing new patients.

Not only do we identify problems, but we also help train front office staff with our proprietary, dental practice-specific **Patient Attraction Phone Training and Certification** course. We're dedicated to helping dentists maximize the number of new patients in their chairs.

Rachel Reeves was SmartBox's Director of Sales in March 2017 when she appeared on our Inside Patient Attraction series. She's moved on to another excellent opportunity in her career, and we wish her all success. Rachel is an expert in helping dental practice front offices appoint many more new patients and was instrumental in the development of our phone training program. She shared her wisdom in this episode.

# Inside Patient Attraction™ March 2017

**Colin:** As a patient attraction company, it's a rare occurrence when I'm going to tell any of our listeners that I can double or even triple your new patients without spending another dime on marketing, but today I'm going to make a rare exception, and I want to show you how to put more butts in your chairs, double or even triple your current new patient flow without spending another dime on marketing or advertising or websites or SEO.

It's great to have you on board, Rachel.

**Rachel:** I'm happy to be here, Colin. Thanks for having me on.

**Colin:** We're going to talk a little bit today about phone training and what it means to these doctors, because it's not really just phone training, you know. We see so many doctors that spend all these thousands and thousands and hundreds of thousands of dollars on marketing, and they never get a return from it. Today, I want to talk about why that is and how having a great front desk can fix that, can play that role of actually making your marketing get more results.

**Rachel:** When we're looking at marketing and how it works, we look at key performance indicators, and for us at SmartBox, number one is calls. Right? When you're looking at how many calls come in, the next thing that you look at is how that person answers the phone and are they able to appoint that prospective patient.

**Colin:** In all the doctors that I've talked to over all the years, I've never once had a doctor that said to me, "Colin, my front desk sucks. They don't appoint any patients. They need training." I've never once had a doctor actually admit that their front desk was bad. Have you ever had that happen to you?

**Rachel:** Not really, per se, them saying that, but I have had them say, "You know, Jessica may need some help," or "It sounds like Sarah, basically, she just doesn't like the world today," or something in that nature, but not specifically their entire staff.

**Colin:** I feel like what happens a lot of times is a lot of doctors, they go through, they do a training course. There's a lot of big-ego phone trainers out there that do a lot of *rah-rah*, and they go through this course, and they get this certificate on the wall, and then *poof*, they're trained, they're done, and they never follow up on it. There's nobody holding that front desk accountable ongoing to make sure that they're still producing the results. What we've designed our program to do is to be an ongoing, certify and keep your staff up-to-date with as many people, your entire front staff certified for life, online curriculum that you can access any time, and we back it up with monitoring your phones, listening to them, and making sure that your staff is held accountable, because if you don't hold people accountable, it doesn't do a whole lot.

**Rachel:** Right. Yeah, I totally agree. I mean, to me it's all about, you can start a conversation with somebody and guide them through to the result and make sure that when they hang up, they feel good about it. That's what SmartBox does. We start with: How are they answering the phone? Do they sound like they just woke up, or do they sound mad because they're hungry? Are you feeding your employees? Are they getting to take a lunch? You know.

**Colin:** You hit an interesting thing there. One of the big hurdles that we see a lot is the front desk taking lunches, because your highest call volume for new patients is going to occur around lunchtime, from 10:30

to 2:30, and when you have front desks that are out for lunch, you have calls not getting answered. New patients aren't going to leave a message.

**Rachel:** No.

**Colin:** They're not going to call you back. They're not going to leave a voicemail for you to check. They're not going to wait around and hope it works out. They're going to go right down that list to the next provider or the next dentist and make a phone call, and you lost them. Some of the most effective practices that I've seen, in terms of appointing patients and training their staff, have a ruthless staff meeting once a week, and they actually pull the recorded calls off the answering machine, and they pick two or three or four recorded calls, and they play them and constructively critique them as a group in the staff meeting on a weekly basis. It's ruthless, but it's constructive, and it's positive, and it's making positive changes—not saying, "Oh, Sally. You suck," but "Sally, hey. You did this, but it would have been better if you'd handled it X, Y, Z."

**Rachel:** Absolutely. Yeah. I think that's crucial, and I think that kind of goes back to the culture of a practice. I think that it's important that you slow down and you realize that one call could be worth—we set an average patient at around $1,500 here at SmartBox, so if somebody doesn't give us that in the information ...

**Colin:** That's for a general dentist.

**Rachel:** That's a general dentist. Now, I would say upward in the way of $4,500 to $6,000 for specialties, but what happens is that when you're talking to that person on the phone, they're not just a prospect for that one specific service. They could bring in their aunt or their cousin or whoever.

**Colin:** Absolutely. Excellent.

**Rachel:** I think of us. My mom has 10 brothers and sisters. If I brought in all of them, you know, that's a huge return.

**Colin:** That's why we're ... I mean, part of our phone training, we're big bat-line proponents. If you don't know the bat-line principle, give us a call and talk to us.

We'll give you a little tidbit without selling you the whole program, but the bat-line concept is critical for new patient scheduling, because you can't be juggling four balls in the air, and then you take that new patient phone call and expect to give them your undivided attention and focus on them and lead to a positive result.

**Rachel:** That's absolutely the truth, and so it's really, to me, it's important to be able to not only control the call but control your own emotions and your own environment, what's going on around you. Things may get busy. You need to be able to stop and give undivided attention to that bat line, per se, because that is a prospective patient that could be bringing in, you know, upward of hundreds or thousands of dollars for the practice.

Now, we don't look at them as dollars. We look at them as people, but it's important, it's really important to realize that if you don't answer that call and to the best of your ability, somebody else will, and they'll persuade them.

**Colin:** Somebody else will. They will. They will. That's

one thing that ... You know, you look at corporate dentistry. You look at the large dental practices that have grown, privately owned, right? Both of them have something in common. They have great systems. They have great training in place. It's not all about the marketing resources and their big gorilla-in-the-room tactic. It's that they do have good training and they do have good systems. Both of those come down to the phones. How are you going to handle and appoint, what's the management structure inside your office, and making sure that you are appointing as close to that optimal number. You know, we shoot for about 80 percent. We want 90 percent of calls to be answered, and we want to appoint 80 percent of the new patients that call. That's our bar.

**Rachel:** Yeah.

**Colin:** If you want that to happen, it comes down to systems and management and training.

**Rachel:** Yeah. I couldn't agree more.

**Colin:** And accountability.

**Rachel:** And accountability. One thing that I actually really love about our brand is that it is a system, so you're working with all of the different components, tactics, capabilities, per se, that will move your business forward.

**Colin:** Mm-hmm.

**Rachel:** To me, it's real important ... I think one of the reasons we're adding this as a capability, per se, to our suite of products is that it's just as important as the beginning part of a consumer's path. It's just as important as the engagement side of things. This is basically where you take them and you nurture them and you move them on.

**Colin:** Absolutely.

**Rachel:** If this doesn't happen, then you're going to miss out. It's a key factor in the consumer's path.

**Colin:** I think one thing that's been a little backwards in the dental industry so far is there are some other industry experts out there that say you should do the phone training first, and that's going to get you new patients, but phone training doesn't make your phone ring. Right?

**Rachel:** Correct.

**Colin:** I think that's something that is a little bit of a misperception in the world: marketing first, and then you move the golf ball down the garden hose, per se. Right?

**Rachel:** Mm-hmm.

**Colin:** As the consumer's path—if you want to call it that—as they're coming toward you advertising, marketing, then phone training, and then interoffice systems, and then you look at your back-end office systems. Right?

**Rachel:** Yeah.

**Colin:** That's the consumer's path for how you need to be training your office, because you got to get the patients in the door. If you get so caught up on the back end and then the front end, your new patient supply dries up and all of a sudden, you have a cash problem, and you don't want that to happen. "Always work consumer path down" is what I practice and preach to our dentists.

**Rachel:** Yeah. I couldn't agree more.

**Colin:** One of the most important parts of the entire phone call that happens between the doctor's office and the patient is the close, right? That point that you actually appoint them. Part of our teaching is based on Robert Cialdini, who many of you watching this are probably familiar with. If you've followed me for any length of time, you know I'm a huge Cialdini fan. It's all about psychology, right? What we call the dual alternative close, saying, "Would you like to come in for an appointment on Tuesday or Wednesday?" You're giving that prospect the choice, but you're really not giving them a choice. "You're coming in to see me either way" is the psychology component of that, and that's critical.

You know you have the greeting and all these different parts that we train and hold your staff accountable for, but then the close is one of the most important parts. Tell me a little bit about that, Rachel.

**Rachel:** The close is extremely important. You're engaging and you're building rapport throughout the entire conversation with the prospective patient, and it's so important that when you get to that point, you know you have them. You have them kind of hooked, and they like you, and they're interacting with you a little bit. At that point, you say, "Great. I'm looking forward to meeting you. Could you come in today, or could you come in tomorrow? I can get you in at 2 o'clock tomorrow. Does that work?" Basically, you're answering questions that they might ask and overcoming questions that could be thrown at you, making them feel more secure as they move forward, because they don't even have to ask. You've already answered it for them.

**Colin:** What kind of results have you seen working with some of our clients with their phone training specifically?

**Rachel:** I've seen great results with a lot of doctors. One of the ones most recently is out of Texas, and they were kind of ... the girls were just not as confident in their approach. Started working with them on, basically, how to kind of lift their tone a little bit and to sound a little bit more abrasive when they're talking and to control the conversation. That helped them tremendously. They went from like setting about 40 percent of the calls that were coming in to setting almost 75 percent of the calls within about a two-and-a-half-month period.

**Colin:** Wow.

**Rachel:** What that means is that relationships do matter. The way you talk to somebody does matter.

**Colin:** How you make them feel.

**Rachel:** How you make them feel. If I answer the phone, and I say, "SmartBox Dental Practice," you know, "This is Rachel," or if I say "SmartBox Dental Practice. This is Rachel. How can I help you?" There's quite a bit of a difference there in how I just greeted that person. It's just really important to be conscientious of the way you sound and, too, of what you say as you move forward in the conversation and listen for just a second to try to understand, What is it that they really need?

Are they needing it now because they're in pain? Are they needing it now because they chipped their front tooth and they're embarrassed? You know, and you shoot right at that.

**Colin:** Back to the results. You said they were at 40 percent, and now they're at 70 percent?

**Rachel:** Them? Yeah, about 75 percent.

**Colin:** An 80 percent increase ...

**Rachel:** Yes.

**Colin:** ... in new patients without another dime spent on marketing. That's just in appointing the calls that are already occurring at a higher percentage.

**Rachel:** Absolutely. Yes.

**Colin:** Well, that's phenomenal.

**Rachel:** It is phenomenal, and that makes my day when that happens, because it means we're doing our job. You know, we don't need to continue to ask for more and more investment to get to move the needle up. You know, we get to help you with that.

**Colin:** I know I was looking at a doctor out of New York that, again, like I said earlier, thinks his call team is so awesome, thinks there's no problems with them. He thinks that they've been trained and they're great, and during business hours, he's answering 40 percent of his phone calls coming in. During business hours.

**Rachel:** Wow.

**Colin:** Unbelievable. It's not always the percentage you're appointing, but I've seen so many doctors that their staff, whether they're understaffed or it's during lunchtime, whatever it may be, they're just flat out not answering calls.

**Rachel:** Yeah. Well, I'd have to give them another one of my sayings, which is, "I love you more than your feelings, doctor, and we need to look at this." That's unacceptable.

**Colin:** Absolutely. Absolutely.

**Rachel:** Yeah. There's always room for improvement. I think with any skill, there's always room for improvement.

**Colin:** Absolutely.

**Rachel:** It's that ability to be humble and willing that will make a huge difference for practices across the United States, is to try something different, and to hold each other accountable. I like that you've said that a few times, because if peers hold each other accountable, just think how much further the practice is going to go. I mean ...

**Colin:** Oh, absolutely.

We're opening up our next training curriculum with the phone training program here in about 45 days, so if anybody has interest in getting on, feel free to give us a call, shoot us an email. Be glad to give you more information about signing up during our next open enrollment period.

**Rachel:** Yeah. I would love to work with some new doctors or existing doctors.

**Colin:** Awesome. Yeah, or existing. Well, it's been great to have you on the show, Rachel.

**Rachel:** Thanks, Colin.

**Colin:** Thanks for coming and hanging out a little bit, and as always, keep moving forward.

Phone tracking is the ideal way to monitor your return on marketing investment. Depending on which phone tracking package you choose—and there are quite a few to choose from—you can also have a database of calls that you can review at your leisure.

If you have any leisure, that is.

## So, You've Got This Database ...

Listening to recordings of your practice calls can help you quickly identify and correct any problems with your front office staff's phone technique.

There's just one small issue: If you attempt to listen to every recorded phone call to your practice, you'll quickly realize that you can kiss your weekends good-bye.

Think about the amount of time your staff spends on the phones during one week. If you're open 40 hours weekly, and one or more staff members is fielding calls just 20 percent of the time, you've got eight hours of recordings to review. **That's one full day with no breaks**.

This is **not** why you got into dentistry, and it's an enormous waste of your time and talents.

Smart dentists who want every appointed new patient possible will outsource call review to a reputable firm. That's a hat you can gladly take off.

Of course, knowing that there's a problem and knowing how to **correct** it are very different things.

Dental practice phone technique wasn't one of your courses in dental school. And while you might be a natural in dealing with new patients over the phone, do you know how to effectively convey what you're doing to your staff?

If you are an effective trainer, congratulations! You just might pull this off.

Now, do you have the time to train your people, monitor their performance on an ongoing basis, and keep making money by seeing patients?

Unless you're a phone training wizard with a good amount of free time, this is another area that you'll be better off outsourcing.

## If All This Is Sounding Like a Tall Order, Don't Worry

Website redesign and optimization; fresh, unique, and authoritative content; social media marketing; online reputation management; email content creation, drip marketing and testing; and phone tracking and phone practice technique training—there's a lot involved in taking, holding, and making the high ground work for you.

**You don't have to do it yourself, and you shouldn't.**

If you'd rather be doing the dentistry than doing your dental marketing—**and** get outstanding results—read on.

> *The two most powerful warriors are patience and time.*
> — Leo Tolstoy

(Hey, it's Tolstoy—what can we say?)

Our daily phone log and recorded calls into our internet phone number we've been very pleased with, and our website is beautiful—you've done one heck of a great job.

— **Dr. Randy Schmidt, Chicago Area**

We have had tremendous results from working with SmartBox and Colin. It has been fun. The relationships we've formed have been great. The favorite thing that has kept me excited is the fact that we can monitor the calls coming in, listen to the calls, and really help our front desk grow in terms of verbal skills, because it's one thing to get the calls, but you've got to convert those calls. That has helped me coach my team a little better.

— **Dr. Travis Watson, Marietta, Georgia**

# "Thrival" Strategies

If you're not tracking your
marketing channels, you're
throwing away money.

Don't rely on patient self-report;
it's been shown to be inaccurate.

Phone tracking is the ideal way to
determine ROI by channel.

Double down on what returns
the most new patients.

The best marketing program is wasted if the
prospect isn't converted to an appointed patient.

Consider dental practice-specific phone
training for your front office.

*I think at the beginning
we talked about doubling
and we'd be happy.*

*And now we're sitting at three or four
times that amount of new patients.*

*SmartBox will generate
the calls for you.*

*You just have to get them
answered and get the patients in.*

— Dr. Anish Patel, Panama City, Florida

# CHAPTER 5

# CALL IN THE ELITE TROOPS: SMARTBOX

*I love it when a plan comes together.*
~ Col. John "Hannibal" Smith, *The A-Team*

(OK, he had help, but still ...)

"I don't have time to put it all together. I want to focus on my patients and focus on what their needs are. I like to tinker with the stuff, but to be honest, I'm not that great at it. So, I wanted to find a company that could do everything, as far as marketing, for me. I decided to make the leap of faith, and I'm glad that I did because I've been very happy with SmartBox and their ability to take all the stuff, put it together, and handle that aspect so I can focus on my patients."
— Dr. Jonathan Gilbart, Hagerstown, Maryland

SmartBox has been very instrumental in the growth of our practice going from 250 to 300 to 350 new patients per month, contributing ideas to us on marketing techniques, helping us evaluate the effectiveness of how much money I'm spend-

ing, and where I should effectively spend that.
— **Dr. Katie Post, Rochester, Minnesota**

Since we've implemented our SmartBox Patient Attraction System, we're definitely getting the quality patients that I want to see come into my practice.
— **Dr. James Kiehl, Nashua, New Hampshire**

I think when we started we were somewhere in the double digits, maybe 70 or 80 new patients a month. Last month we had 257. We've been with the program two or three years. It works. The numbers just start to tick up through their Facebook posts, and website, and updates, and things like that.
— **Dr. Anish Patel, Panama City, Florida**

Actually, the number of visits to my website is down during the time that I'm collecting a lot more money, so we've extrapolated that information from more visits, less money, to less visits, higher quality patient, more collections. It's working.
— **Dr. Ron Receveur, New Albany, Indiana**

Before we went live with SmartBox, we had one practice location, and at that time, we were getting about 20 new patient opportunities a month. Now, 11 months later, we have two practice locations and we're averaging about 70 to 75 new patient opportunities a month. It's been a big increase for us, and it's all due to the targeted marketing that SmartBox has done for us.
— **Dr. Dick Davenport, Laredo, Texas**

After I did one of the webinars, I really felt confident that you guys knew what you were doing, and that you could take me from point A to point

B with virtually no pain on my part and relatively little involvement on my part. And that's important to me because I don't have time to become an expert; I've gotta be a dentist, I've gotta be a business owner.

— **Dr. Ryan Shepherd, Albuquerque, New Mexico**

It's far easier to sleep at night knowing the future of my practice is on firm ground.

—**Dr. Randy Schmidt, Chicago Area**

What you've just finished reading in the preceding chapters are the four steps of SmartBox's **industry-leading Patient Attraction System**™—Attraction, Conversion, Follow-Up, and Tracking.

It's fair to say that SmartBox **pioneered** the idea of higher ground for dentists. We work with more than 550 dentists on three continents to help them get **more and better patients**. There's a lot of emphasis on getting more patients, but as you've learned, getting better patients—your higher ground—is essential to your success.

Dr. Thomas J. Feder of Belleville, Illinois, became a SmartBox dentist and saw a significant increase in better patients. He told us, "Our average case value has increased. People are coming in looking for dentures and implants. The practice is now overwhelming our dental lab."

But yes, we also help dental practices get more patients overall. We provide a consistent stream of new patients so our doctors can focus on doing the dentistry.

**And doing the dentistry is what makes you money, after all.**

Our **Patient Attraction System**™ includes everything discussed in this book, and much more.

- HIPAA-compliant dental website design
- Dental online marketing
- Dental video production
- Dental email marketing
- Dental search engine optimization
- Dental review monitoring & review solicitation
- Dental social media marketing
- Dental SEM and paid online advertising

## Let's Get a Better Look

Sometimes, you just need an eagle's-eye view to put things together. That's what Trent Arkema, SmartBox's Vice President of Marketing, provided when he appeared in this episode of the Inside Patient Attraction™ webinar series.

If you're looking for a concise overview of the Patient Attraction System™, this is for you.

## Inside Patient Attraction™ June 2017

**Colin:** Welcome to Inside Patient Attraction. I'm Colin Receveur, and today's ultra-competitive online environment means you have to step up your game if you want to play. I'm going to be joined today by Trent Arkema, our Vice President of Marketing. And we're going to talk all about what you need to be doing to dominate your market area, stay ahead of the competition, beat corporate dentistry, and more. Stay tuned.

Trent, thanks for being on the show.

**Trent:** Thank you for having me. It's a pleasure to be here.

**Colin:** Awesome, awesome. So, I want to talk today a little bit about digital marketing. You're the VP of Marketing here at SmartBox. And what do you see in traditional dental marketing, when we bring a client in, what kind of issues and problems do you typically see with their marketing that they and we both recognize need to be fixed?

**Trent:** Yeah, I mean, a lot of the dentists that we worked with—I've been doing traditional marketing, and that's really print advertising and really focused on coupons and specials and discounts. They've dabbled in a little bit of digital, but they don't have an integrated approach.

**Colin:** When you say integrated approach, what's that mean? That's kind of a buzzword in the world today.

**Trent:** Yeah, I mean, it's really about being everywhere that the user is. You just can't be in one spot. Now that the user is so connected and so wired all the time, as an advertiser and as a business, you need to be where your patients are.

**Colin:** So, if a dentist were to want to see what an integrated, all-encompassing approach might look like in their market area, say, what maybe one of their competitors is doing, would it be probably a safe bet that if you look at your local corporate dentist, you could see all the money that big gorilla is going around spending?

**Trent:** Yeah, I mean, the corporate dentists do have bigger pockets than a smaller dentistry. They're going to see whatever they're doing. If you're just doing the basic things and going after the coupons and the specials, it's really a race to a bottom. You're not doing anything that any other dentist isn't doing and every other dentist has a master's too. You're not standing apart. It's just a race to the bottom. You're going to get less patients down the road overall because again, you don't stand out in any aspect of your marketing.

**Colin:** It's really hard, too, for the private fee-for-service dentist with one practice to compete on price with the corporate dentist that has the economies of scale. They can undercut you on everything because they have cheaper labs, they have cheaper supplies, they have bigger advertising budgets. Overall, they bring a big-business economic approach to the small-town dentistry world.

**Trent:** Exactly, exactly. And so, when you look at things, if you're going to try to compete on price, again, you're probably going to end up losing, and that's why in the digital world, with all the different tools and platforms that you can use, digital is really the way to go and get patients because you can do it cost-effectively.

**Colin:** And when you talk about an integrated approach, tell me a little bit about the different steps or the different—what we call the "pillars" here. I want to talk a little bit with our webinar viewers about what four steps and four items we talk about here internally, our Four Pillars. Let's walk our viewers through why those are important. Does that sound good?

**Trent:** Definitely, definitely.

**Colin:** So, Pillar One, Attraction. What is Attraction and what is that about?

**Trent:** Yeah, really, we're talking about a system when we talk about the Four Pillars. We're not talking about going to chase patients. We're talking about attracting patients. And that's done through a system, as you mentioned.

Really, Attraction is about being everywhere your users are at, having that integrated approach. Having been in organic, being in paid search, being on Facebook, being in display advertising through the Google Display Network, really encompassing everywhere somebody could be from a digital landscape is where you need to be because users are going to enter that funnel at different points and on different devices. It's important that you be everywhere at all times as well.

**Colin:** When you're basically just talking about dominating your marketplace ...

**Trent:** Exactly.

**Colin:** ... being seen everywhere in the online sphere.

**Trent:** Right, exactly.

**Colin:** When a potential new patient—you call them users, but let's be real specific. These are actual new patients that are out there searching. They're going to see you no matter where they go. If they're on Facebook, they're going to get retargeted. If they're on Google, they're going to get hit. If they're on Bing, they're going to get hit. If they're searching, if they're in their email box, you're going to be delivering messages to them on some kind of regular basis, not so often that you're annoying them, but enough that you're keeping your name in front of them and conditioning them with that trust until they're ready to move forward.

**Trent:** Right. The second pillar is Conversion. Once

they've done their research, they've found you, they've read reviews about you and so, it's really important to have that social trust that you built through online reviews and having reviews on your website as well, so people have that trust factor. They're going to take that next step and convert, whether that be through a phone call from your website, whether they've looked you up on Yelp or anything else, that phone number appears there or a Google review, but also through a form submission on your website as well.

You have to have multiple conversion points so users can convert however they want to convert with you. That is really the second pillar. In order to be there and convert that user, again, you have to be there organically, from a paid search perspective, and constantly working with them and reminding them through email follow-up as well.

Also with Conversion, we want to have video testimonials. Those are huge. People seeing ... other patients work with the doctor helps solidify that doctor and builds that trust as well. Video testimonials and having videos onsite is a huge part of that conversion aspect as well.

**Colin:** You know, one of the biggest things about Conversion, and I think in marketing, we get caught up in the Conversion aspect of it and we need to make sure we realize that Conversion is converting real people into patients, in the butts in the chairs. In order to take this prospect over here and move them into the chair or into a phone call, you've got to get them to know, like, and trust you.

Sometimes that happens instantly, but oftentimes,

in dentistry being a very trust-based profession, you have to build that trust. It doesn't happen overnight. If you're just trying to get in patients for cleanings and X-rays and exams, it's a very low level of trust. If you're trying to attract patients that want to spend five grand on Invisalign or they want to spend 10 grand on veneers or $25,000 in implants, that trust level rises with the transaction size.

**Trent:** Definitely. That's where the third pillar comes in. It's about Follow-Up. You just can't stop at Conversion just because somebody picks up that phone and calls you or submits that form. That's not the end of that conversation. That's the beginning of your conversation with them.

What we do with our dentists is that we have follow-up drip sequences through email. We're constantly following up with that potential patient on things that are important to them. Through that initial contact, we found out, What are they interested in, what is the service that they need? And then follow up with them through a series of emails until they do convert into that patient.

Follow-Up is definitely key just to keep that conversation going and to your point, further build that trust that you've established early on in the relationship.

**Colin:** I think the important thing, Trent, with the email follow-up in this third pillar that we're talking about is you've got to build that trust over time, like I mentioned. You've got to continue to stay in front of these patients, sometimes for six months, before they're ready to buy. Again, with trust level, trust level and transaction size are very relevant, directly proportional to each other, and that also is directly proportional, I think, to the time it takes to build that rapport with that patient.

To get somebody to come in for a $25,000 implant case, that takes a lot of trust and that also takes a significant amount of time to build that trust up, in communication.

**Trent:** Definitely. Yeah, we will basically change how many times we communicate and how frequently we will communicate with a certain patient depending on what services they're interested in. To your point, that drip email sequence could last two weeks or it could last six months with a number of different emails to build that trust and get that patient to convert.

**Colin:** Then, you can also really mix the second and third pillars, where in the second pillar of Conversion, you're going to have patient testimonial videos. You're going to have online reviews that are building that credibility, social proof, what Cialdini talks about as his weapons of influence.

You can also use those in your Follow-Up to continue to drive home the rapport and the image, the expert status that you want to have to your patients in all that follow-up material that you're doing.

**Trent:** Definitely, definitely. You want that message to be consistent, from Conversion to Follow-up and back to Conversion. It's very important that whether you do that through e-books or white papers, that you're having that consistent message across all the different communication channels.

**Colin:** Summing all these up, we're doing Attraction,

we're doing Conversion, we're doing Follow-Up—how do we make sense of all of these and figure out ... I mean, how do we know what to do and what not to do?

**Trent:** Yeah, I think, that goes in the fourth pillar, which might be the most important, and that's Tracking. It's about seeing what everything we did in those first three pillars, what that resulted in. We have a very robust tracking system. We have phone call tracking. We have form tracking and we can do that by source so we know where the traffic is coming from, what is actually converting. We can do more of what is getting patients and butts in chairs.

Really, once we have the marketing in place and we have that going for a certain amount of time, we start to read those results. We have call analysts that are listening to every single call as well so we know if there's issues, we can relay to the doctors very quickly, but we're also using that information to continuously optimize our campaigns and make them better, so we're only bidding on the keywords that get you those patients.

We're using your budget as most efficiently as we can. Again, it's continuous optimization through our tracking process that we have in place.

**Colin:** When you say source-level tracking, what do you mean by that? That sounds kind of buzzish. Can you make that sound simple for our docs that are listening?

**Trent:** Right. Early on we talked about Attraction— that you want to be in the Googles, in the Bings, in the Facebooks, in the Google Display Network, and we have tracking set up so we can see what source that user came from, whether that'd be Bing, whether that'd be Google. We don't know starting out whether what's that going to be, so we want to put tracking in place so we can see the results of our advertising efforts and marketing efforts. And then we can do more of that based on the results that we see, so that's what we mean by source-level tracking.

**Colin:** You're able to determine the source of the phone call, being it organic or paid search or email or Facebook or wherever that source of that new patient came from. We can break that down for the doctor and tell them, "Here's how many calls came in, here's how many you're scheduled, here's how many your front desk didn't schedule," and then maybe even the most egregious violation of all, "Here's how many phone calls you didn't even answer during business hours."

**Trent:** Correct. That is very correct.

**Colin:** I did a podcast a couple of months ago talking about phone tracking, and we really got in depth there that if somebody wanted to learn more, we can do that. But from what you've seen, how many doctors don't even answer phone calls during business hours?

**Trent:** That's funny that you brought that up. We were looking at that stat just the other day. There's around 50 percent of the calls that we generate go unanswered by our practices, which is a huge amount when you think about it.

**Colin:** 50 percent?

**Trent:** 50 percent.

**Colin:** Wow. That's not good. That's turning away patients right on your front doorstep.

**Trent:** Exactly.

**Colin:** Trent, we've covered a whole lot of ground here today. What can dentists do right now to implement what we've talked about here? Is this something that they can take and run with today and see some results tomorrow?

**Trent:** Yeah, they can. Some marketing and practices do have the pieces in place to create their own system. A lot of people don't, though, a lot of the dentists don't have the time and don't have the resources to put this in place. We've talked about a lot of things.

We find that some practices dabble in organic or dabble in paid search, but to have that truly integrated system takes a lot of resources, and it doesn't take just one person. It takes a team similar to what SmartBox offers our clients. Really, if you want to have an attraction system and do it full-time, you need a team behind you to really implement that strategy. And we find that few practices really have that.

**Colin:** I think a lot of practices in the one- to two- or three-million-dollar range don't even have marketing people that work in-house. The doctor is wearing the marketing hat. The doctor is wearing the clinician hat. The doctor is wearing the manager hat and doing it all. And you're right. They can't possibly set things up. They just don't have enough hours in the day.

**Trent:** Correct.

**Colin:** For those doctors that are watching and want to see how you stack up against what we're talking about here, our Patient Attraction System™, I'd encourage you to just give us a call. We're glad to give you a complimentary blueprint if you're serious about what a Patient Attraction System can do for your practice in your market area with your patient base, your demographics, what kind of results we've seen in other identical practices to yours. Give us a call at the number on the screen. We'll be glad to set you up, give you an idea of what we can see and our strategy for your practice. And if you like what you see, we can help you do it.

Trent, thanks for being on the show. Appreciate it, sharing some tidbits of your wisdom with everybody here.

**Trent:** Thanks for having me. It was a pleasure.

**Colin:** Stay tuned for the next episode. Thanks for being here. Keep moving forward.

## It's Up to You

So now, you're at a decision point. You can continue to occupy and battle for the low ground while it erodes beneath you. Or you can choose to move to high ground where the better patients are—the patients you want and need to grow your practice.

Dr. Travis Watson of Marietta, Georgia, moved to the high ground. Here's how he describes his experience:

> Ever since we've been working with SmartBox, which was two and a half years ago, we have seen a tremendous return on our investment. It can be daunting sometimes when you take on a new investment and you're changing things. Your staff can be anxious, but as soon as the first few months went by, our staff started to understand why we made this in-

vestment. It's been nothing but great in terms of getting the new patients, and not only getting the new patients, but prequalifying the patient.

Of course, that's just one dentist's experience, but it's echoed time and time again by dentists on three continents. Those are dentists who dared greatly and are succeeding greatly. And **they** get to spend their time doing the dentistry, not ramrodding every aspect of their dental marketing.

If you're ready to act to safeguard your dental practice **and** get more and better patients than you ever have, here's your next step.

**Visit www.PracticeDiscovery.com** to reserve your **free, no-obligation Practice Discovery Session**™. Invest 25 minutes of your time, and we'll show you what our **Patient Attraction System**™ can do for your dental practice.

We'll take the results of that phone call and send you your personalized **Patient Attraction Roadmap**™— again, absolutely free.

## I'll Even Sweeten the Deal

SmartBox is serious about our doctors' success. So much so that we're incentivizing our dentists' front offices to appoint **every new patient caller possible**. And it won't cost the docs a dime.

The **SmartBox $25,000 Challenge** went live in January 2018 and will continue through the end of the year. We're ponying up the prize money out of our own pocket to help our dentists be as successful as possible.

SmartBox will get your phone ringing, but appointing new patients is up to each dentist's front office. Our hard data indicates that far too many incoming calls go unanswered, and too many new prospects are never appointed. That's a **complete** waste of dentist's hard-earned marketing dollars. So we decided to do something about the problem, and the **SmartBox Challenge** was born.

We've created a level playing field for practices of every size and in every market. Here's how it works.

We record every incoming call to our dentists' offices, and our dedicated team of Call Quality Analysts listen to every call. We know how many new patient calls our dentists' offices receive and how many of those prospects are turned into appointed patients.

The challenge winners (we're providing quarterly and annual prizes) are the practices that have the highest average of two scores: the Call Answer Rate and Scheduling Conversion Rate.

So, we're asking doctors' front offices to do two things: answer more calls and appoint more new clients. The quarterly winners will receive gift cards worth hundreds of dollars (we have **thousands** of dollars in gift cards on hand).

Those are good, but the annual prizes are **great**!

- The annual top prize is a $10,000 all-inclusive vacation for a practice's staff.

- The annual second prize is a $5,000 getaway to Las Vegas for a practice's staff.

- The annual third prize is a $2,000 spa package for a practice's staff.

Every SmartBox dentist is automatically entered in the contest, but it takes a full quarter of results to be eligible.

Let me put it this way: **We're at least as serious about your success as you are**. The **SmartBox $25,000 Challenge** benefits you, your practice, and your staff. It's a win all around. Are you and your staff up to the challenge?

# One Quick Takeaway

As a final thought, let's hear from someone with a great deal of experience when it comes to conflicts: General Omar N. Bradley.

> **This is as true in everyday life as it is in battle: we are given one life and the decision is ours whether to wait for circumstances to make up our mind, or whether to act, and in acting, to live.**

I wish you all success, Doctor.

> I'm not all that savvy on the internet with marketing and things like that. I just know that's not my thing. I liked what Colin had to say. We got in touch with SmartBox and felt like we needed to make that change, so we left our other marketing expert and turned to you guys, and we're happy we did.
>
> — **Dr. Lawrence Fox, Burke, Virginia**

> Our case size was $2,500 per new patient. Since SmartBox, it has quickly grown to now $3,100. Give Colin Receveur a try. You won't be sorry.
>
> — **Dr. Mitchel Friedman, Lincroft, New Jersey**

I think that the numbers are just going to keep going up. Now that we have our new facility, we're going to 300-400 new patients a month, I'm sure—by the end of the year, hopefully. I think at the beginning we talked about doubling and we'd be happy, and now we're sitting at three or four times that amount of new patients. SmartBox will generate the calls for you. You just have to get them answered and get the patients in.

— **Dr. Anish Patel, Panama City, Florida**

Web marketing is truly Colin's passion. When a person is truly passionate about something, it shows in their work. He's on top of all the latest up-to-the-minute changes in the virtual world, which is necessary as fast as everything is changing. He's sensitive to what things cost and tries to explain to you what methods or techniques give you the most "bang for your buck."

— **Dr. Ron Receveur, New Albany, Indiana**

# CHAPTER 6

# CASES IN POINT

*That some achieve great
success, is proof to all
that others can achieve it as well.*
~ **Abraham Lincoln**

(Yeah, what he said.)

> Since 2002 to 2008, my practice was slowly growing. Unfortunately, when you looked at the total collections for the practice, it had been at 2.1 million when I came and slowly had dropped every year, and the year I bought in, it was at 1.8 million."
> —**Dr. Katie Post, Rochester, Minnesota**

Let me begin this chapter by stating that Dr. Post's fortunes have turned around since she chose SmartBox. I could present her as a case study due to the outstanding success she enjoys now.

The thing about case studies, though, is that they're snapshots. They "freeze" what happened within a certain time frame. But that doesn't tell you what's likely to happen going forward.

Any case study study is illustrative at best—not definitive. But there's value in case studies because they illustrate the **possible**, and point the way to you achieving **equal or better results**.

To make the following case studies as useful to you as possible, I've included a lot of background information, including revenue figures over successive years. The doctors in these case studies have agreed to allow their information to be used, but they prefer not to be named.

You can compare your current situation to these doctors' previous statuses point by point. No two dental practices are identical, and you might have to extrapolate a bit to fit these examples to your own situation.

But you'll find yourself. And when you do, you might just find the solution to the challenges your practice faces.

---

# Case Study #1
# Local Doc Makes Good

**Location:** Northeast U.S.
**Core Market Base (within 5 miles):** ~ 70,000 people
**Practice:** Single-dentist, general dentistry
**Longevity:** 11 years
**Main Revenue Streams:** Cleanings and exams; restorations; teeth whitening; Invisalign
**Highest Historical Annual Revenue:** $970K
**2015 Revenues:** $720K
**SmartBox Start Date:** February 2016
**2016 Revenues:** $860K
**2017 Revenues:** $1.13M
**Competitors:** 9 small general dental practices;

2 orthodontic practices; 2 corporate offices (Aspen Dental, Perfect Dental); 1 implant practice

---

Dr. G is a 30-something general practice dentist. He and his wife live with their two children in a medium-sized county in the Northeast.

When he opened practice 11 years ago, his market included a total of nine established dental practices. Now, he has 14 competitors, and the 50 percent increase in competition has taken a toll on his earnings.

"I wouldn't say that I had it all my way when we opened," he said. "But for the number of people in our area, there weren't all that many dental practices. We had no problem getting people through the door until about four years ago. That's when two other general dentists went into practice. And Aspen Dental opened up a year later. We saw a small hit almost immediately in our new patient numbers. And some of our existing patients went to those new practices, too."

He added, "Sometimes I wonder whether we delivered a good enough experience for those patients who deserted us. I made retaining our patient base a priority, but our efforts to increase loyalty have only slowed the loss, not stopped it. Some of those patients were marginal in terms of their value to the practice, but they had value. Now, some other dentist is making money on them, not me."

Things took a turn for the much worse when a major employer unexpectedly closed, leaving about 1,500 people unemployed. "We probably lost a hundred or more patients when that happened," he said. "The company that shut down wasn't far from our location, and that made us really convenient for patients. A lot of those people moved out of town to find work."

Over the last four years, Dr. G's revenues slipped from a high of $970K to $720K at the end of 2015, but it wasn't all due to patient loss. "There's always been a price war in town," he commented. "It was usually a kind of hit-or-miss thing. Somebody would offer a limited-time $59 cleaning and exam. Another dentist would advertise five bucks cheaper. That kind of thing. But now, Aspen and Perfect Dental have constant low price points. That's hurt. I never used to have to spend much on marketing, but nowadays it's a must-do."

Dr. G managed to maintain his staff, in part by shopping for lower-cost suppliers and streamlining for efficiency. But he was worried about the future. "I have a great crew. Most of them have been with me from the beginning, and they've all pitched in to make my practice successful. But if this downward trend continues, I'm going to have to cut staff, even though it would break my heart."

As you've guessed by now, Dr. G read the writing on the wall and decided to do things differently. His sign-on date with SmartBox was February 6, 2016.

## What SmartBox Did for Dr. G

Dr. G's situation is one that's well-known to the experts at SmartBox. The first thing we did was work with him to establish his practice goals. The major goals were:

1. **Increase year-over-year revenues:** The doctor is shooting for $1 million-plus.

2. **Increase average case value by 15 percent:** For Dr. G, this would be a bump from $1,500 to $1,725.

3. **Increase existing patient base by 20 percent:** Including patients who are "infrequent flyers" at the practice, the increase would be from 1,200 to 1,440.

4. **Maintain a steady new patient stream:** Dr. G wanted at least 20 more new patients per month to offset an average annual attrition rate of around 13 percent.

SmartBox did a demographic analysis of his market and even visited the area to get eyes on the ground, so to speak. We analyzed his practice location, toured the office, spoke with the staff, and performed a competitor analysis.

Dr. G provided the information about his practice and services that we needed to create his new, state-of-the-art website. That website, supplemented by expertly written and optimized new patient content, launched a little over three months from his sign-on. (It should be noted that Dr. G was and continues to be very cooperative in getting us information and meeting with his Client Success Manager at least monthly.)

Shortly after the website launch, we established Dr. G on Facebook, Google My Business, and Twitter. His website featured a blog with ongoing fresh and unique content produced by SmartBox, including new quizzes, infographics, videos, and long-form posts every month.

We revisited the practice after the website launch to record his doctor videos and numerous patient testimonials, which were quickly edited, optimized for the web, and posted to his website. We also got him his own YouTube channel to broaden those videos' reach.

Given his market, we also produced a series of display ads and one postcard campaign to coordinate with the website launch.

There was a lot more that happened behind the scenes—pay-per-click (PPC) ads, promoted Facebook and Twitter posts, ongoing website optimization, email content streams and automated email marketing, phone tracking and call monitoring, and more.

### Dr. G Reports

"I can't believe it," he told us, shaking his head. "I've never seen growth like this. We're up a third in revenue in just two years. I won't say our phone is ringing off the hook, but at SmartBox's suggestion I hired another staff member just to handle calls. We're now appointing many more new patients, and our chairs are almost always full. If this keeps up, I'll have to hire an associate, and I had nearly given up hope of ever being able to do that."

Dr. G is on track with his growth curve and his revenue goals. But what about his case value? "We're getting new patients who want more than bare-bones dentistry," he said. "We haven't quite hit that 15 percent increase in average case value—I think it was 13 percent as of a few months ago—but I know we'll get there. We might even go higher."

Dr. G trusted SmartBox to move his practice to higher ground, and he's positioned to reap the benefits for many more years to come.

---

# Case Study #2
# The Four Little Operatories
# That Could

**Location:** Southern U.S.

**Core Market Base (within 5 miles):** > 260,000 people
**Practice:** Two-dentist, general dentistry
**Longevity:** 15 years
**Main Revenue Streams:** Cleanings and exams; restorations; teeth whitening; Invisalign and braces; minor cosmetic dentistry
**Highest Historical Annual Revenue:** $1.7M
**2016 Revenues:** $1.3M
**SmartBox Start Date:** March 2017
**2017 Revenues:** $1.53M
**Projected 2018 Revenues:** $1.86M
**Competitors:** 15 small general dental practices; 3 multi-dentist practices; 4 orthodontic practices; 2 endodontic practices; 4 corporate practices (2 Aspen Dentals, ClearChoice, Kool Smiles); 2 private implant practices

---

Dr. R is a dentist in his 40s who opened the practice and ran it as a solo dentist until five years ago. At that time, the demands on his time became so great that he was forced to expand his staff, hiring several front-office people and signing on an associate dentist, Dr. L.

The high revenue period for the practice occurred between 2012 and 2013. As of 2016, revenue had declined by 22 percent. When asked what caused their growth curve to head south, Dr. R. shook his head.

"I'm still trying to figure that out," he said. "I think our services are competitive in breadth and cost. We've got good presence in the community. Our website, I think, is pretty good. We do some mailers and the occasional newspaper ad. And the practice implemented a patient referral program that was good for a while until ... I don't know what happened, but referrals just fell off."

When Dr. L joined the practice, things quickly picked up until there simply weren't enough operatories to meet the demand. Appointment times were being pushed too far back, and the doctors needed to expand the physical plant. Fortunately, there was a solution.

"We're lucky in our location. Dr. R owns the land, and we had the space where we could physically expand the practice by adding four more operatories," Dr. L explained. "The construction phase was a royal pain, but things were so much better afterward. But then the bottom fell out, and we were left with a $300,000 construction loan as well as our usual overhead."

Some questioning revealed that the competitive landscape had changed considerably after Dr. L became an associate.

"Yeah, Aspen came in around 2014," Dr. R said, "and there were a couple of other practices that opened within, what? Eighteen months or so? And since then, the competition has just kind of ticked up year over year. We recognized that fairly early, and we ran some specials and discounts to drum up new business. It worked for a while, and now it just seems like we're throwing money away."

Dr. L agreed. "We're just not getting enough new patients through the doors. And the ones we do get either want the cheapest solution for their problems, or they want to beat us up on price for more complex procedures."

## What SmartBox Did for Dr. R and Dr. L

When the dentists began talking with SmartBox, they were extremely wary. They'd been burned (their term) by a previous dental marketing company that promised the moon but delivered very little.

Still, they knew that they had to change the trajectory of their practice, so they were willing to talk. Smart-Box reviewed their website and discovered that it was generations out of date. The last revision in content and SEO was in 2011, and the site took far too long to load. To make matters worse, the design was hopelessly dated.

We also furnished them with some statistics about declining urban newspaper readership, and they quickly realized why their display ads had failed to produce.

The doctors signed on with SmartBox in March 2017. Their main practice goals were:

1. **Increase year-over-year revenue by 17 percent:** Starting with 2016's low of $1.3 million, the compounding effect of 17 percent annual growth put them on track for revenues of $2.09 million by 2020.

2. **Increase average case value by 19 percent from $1,300 to $1,547:** The doctors' case value had declined markedly as they were undercut by increased competition. In SmartBox's experience, this increase was a very conservative goal.

3. **Increase monthly new patient numbers by 24 percent:** In contrast, that's an ambitious goal, but the practice has the bandwidth to accommodate an increase in new patients, from 2,200 to 2,728 annually.

4. **Pay off their construction loan:** Both doctors were very unhappy that they hadn't been able to pay down the loan in the time frame they'd envisioned, saying it felt like an anchor around their necks.

SmartBox started with the practice website, which was making the doctors largely invisible online. Launching a new website requires considerable cooperation from the practice, and there were delays. The new site didn't go live until July 2017, leaving just five months in the calendar year to generate new patients.

Between them, Dr. R and Dr. L have complementary skills sets. Dr. R has postgraduate training in orthodontics, and Dr. L has training in cosmetic dentistry. Both doctors are very personable as well.

SmartBox's content team worked to position the doctors and the practice as the go-to location for a host of expert dental services and a superior patient experience. That approach was uniformly carried out on their new website, in their social media, and in the paid ad campaigns that SmartBox produced and managed.

## The Doctors Report

"We saw a sharp increase in new patients within a month of our site going live," Dr. L said. "I think we got like 35 or 40 more new patients than normal that first month, and it's increased from there. But what's even better is that we're getting people who don't argue about price! I don't think we've run the numbers for 2017, but I know our average case value is up."

Dr. R noted a new trend that was both gratifying and a little alarming. "We had people coming in who said, 'I never knew you guys were here!' It's great that they found us. It's not so great that I obviously didn't realize how bad our old website was."

With their SmartBox Patient Attraction System™ operational for just five months, the practice revenues still increased from $1.3 million in 2016 to **$1.53 million** in 2017. That's a **16 percent** increase in less than half a year's operation.

And that construction loan? "We aim to be free of that debt in 18 months," Dr. L said. "And this time, I know we'll make that happen. We're both feeling very good about where our practice is now."

# Case Study #3
# A Tale of 3 Dentists

**Location:** Midwest
**Core Market Base (within 5 miles):** > 400,000 people
**Practice:** Three-dentist, general dentistry
**Longevity:** 14 years
**Main Revenue Streams:** Cleanings and exams; restorations, including implant restorations; teeth whitening; periodontal disease treatment; Invisalign and braces; cosmetic dentistry (veneers, Snap-On Smile®, dental bonding)
**Highest Historical Annual Revenue:** $2.6M
**2015 Revenues:** $2.0M
**SmartBox Start Date:** January 2016
**2016 Revenues:** $2.4M
**2017 Revenues:** $2.91M
**Projected 2018 Revenues:** $3.63M
**Competitors:** 19 small general dental practices; 5 multi-dentist practices; 6 orthodontic practices; 3 endodontic practices; 6 corporate practices (2 Aspen Dentals, ClearChoice, 2 Heartland Dentals, Kool Smiles); 3 private implant practices; 2 periodontal practices

In this metro area, dental competition is the name of the game. Drs. K, C, and M know that all too well.

The "three amigos," as they call themselves, met during dental school. After brief stints in other practices, they reunited to form their own practice in 2004. To say that things have changed for them would be an understatement.

"The number of general and specialty practices in our market has doubled since we opened," said Dr. M. "Even adjusting for inflation, we're spending a lot more on our marketing and not getting nearly enough return."

"We were one of the first smaller practices to offer treatment for advanced periodontal disease," added Dr. K. "It was a major advantage when we opened. Now, we're going head-to-head against two specialty practices."

After reaching an all-time high of $2.6 million in revenue, the practice has watched its success diminish year after year. But they certainly haven't taken the development lying down.

"We've probably worked with four or five marketing firms," Dr. C remarked. "I'd describe the results as mixed at best. Sure, we had some good months, but we had some terrible months, too. And believe me, those firms' services didn't come cheap. We finally gave up and started doing our own marketing. That was a pain. It took a lot of after-hours time."

Dr. M added, "We had a lot more money to throw at our marketing once we started doing it ourselves. But I wouldn't say that our results, in terms of the quantity and quality of new patients we got, were much better than [what] the marketing companies produced. It just wasn't enough."

## What SmartBox Did for Drs. K, C, and M

SmartBox began by doing a market and competitor analysis. The competitor analysis included a deep dive into competitors' marketing practices compared to those of Drs. K, C, and M.

Our analysis showed that the three amigos weren't taking full advantage of their strengths and their inclusive approach to dentistry. Theirs is a comprehensive practice that offers a lot of convenience and continuity of care for patients.

Basically, they weren't using their strengths to stand out in a crowded market. Refocusing their marketing to capitalize on those strengths would give them much more name recognition.

With those realizations, the doctors named these as their three top marketing goals:

1. **Stop the bleeding:** Realize year-over-year revenue growth of 10-15 percent.

2. **Enhance income from specialty revenue streams:** Boost income from implants and implant restorations, periodontal disease treatment, Invisalign, and cosmetic dentistry.

3. **Increase market share:** Gain 5-10 percent new market share.

Within 90 days of signing, SmartBox launched the practice's new website. In marked contrast to the previous website, the new site emphasized the benefits of receiving treatment from **these** doctors and the high-quality experience patients could expect.

Significantly, all their marketing was revised to accommodate prospects' general education level and understanding of dental procedures and outcomes. The previous site was heavy on dental jargon and focused on the doctors' postgraduate training.

The practice's Facebook page underwent the same radical shift in approach, and the staff began responding much more quickly to Facebook and Twitter posts.

Most importantly, SmartBox helped the doctors realize that they were losing a lot of patients at the point of initial contact—the phone. They elected to have their front office staff undergo SmartBox's Patient Attraction Phone Training & Certification course.

## The Doctors Report

"Working with SmartBox has been a real game-changer for our practice," said Dr. M. "Implant cases are way up, and we're also doing a lot more, and more involved, cosmetic dentistry."

"The growth in revenue has been amazing," Dr. C added. "I never dreamed we could experience 20 percent year-over-year growth. But the trajectory is clear, and we're headed for an all-time high in revenue this year. One million over our previous best year is nothing to sneeze at."

"I think the best thing that has come out of working with SmartBox is that we feel like the practice is sustainable," said Dr. K. "Our marketing is on a different level than our competition, and I expect that we'll be able to retain the advantage we enjoy now. I know that the three of us could never have done what Colin and his people have done, and I doubt that any of our competitors could manage it."

# Case Study #4
# Let's Get a Couple of Things Straight

**Location:** Eastern U.S.
**Core Market Base (within 5 miles):** > 750,000 people
**Practice:** Four-doctor orthodontic group
**Longevity:** 20 years
**Main Revenue Streams:** Braces—traditional, clear, ceramic, and colored; Invisalign
**Highest Historical Annual Revenue:** $4.5M
**2016 Revenues:** $3.7M
**SmartBox Start Date:** February 2017
**2017 Revenues:** $4.2M
**Projected 2018 Revenues:** $4.95M
**Competitors:** 11 orthodontic practices; 24 general dentistry practices offering Invisalign and/or ClearCorrect

Recent estimates are that some 45 percent of people are unhappy with the alignment of their teeth. Twenty percent or more of people would consider orthodontic treatment.

You'd think that in a city of more than two million people, it wouldn't be hard for an orthodontic practice to find new patients. That was true for Drs. O, S, B, and V for many years, but increased competition has reversed the growth trend of their practice.

"Things went bad in 2015," Dr. V said. "This was already a very competitive market, but that was the year that four new general practices opened. All of those dentists immediately began offering Invisalign, and it didn't take long for that to begin to hurt our bottom line."

Practice revenue dropped 18 percent in a single year, and for those doctors, it was a wake-up call.

"Clear aligners had become a mainstay revenue stream for our practice," said Dr. S. "We still got our share of traditional braces and the newer variants, but those dentists were undercutting our price on clear aligners consistently. We knew that we'd have to do something different to remain competitive."

"We looked around at the various dental marketing firms out there, and our consensus was that SmartBox was our best bet," said Dr. O. "I saw an ad on Dental-town for 'The Ultimate Case Start Solution,' and I ordered it. Heck, it was free. Once we'd had a chance to go over SmartBox's approach to getting more and better new patients, the decision to sign up was a no-brainer."

Dr. B wasn't so sure at first. "We'd been disappointed by dental marketing companies before. They just didn't get dental patients. A couple of us would like to retire within seven to 10 years. Given the way that things were going, we didn't have time to take a chance on an unproven marketing firm. But when I read that Colin is the son of dentist, and that SmartBox deals exclusively with dental practices, I agreed to give them a try."

The practice signed on with SmartBox in February 2017, and we got to work.

The four doctors' goals for the practice were:

1. **Increase the number of clear aligner case starts:** The doctors were interested in a 25 percent gain.

2. **Attract more new patients who had higher discretionary income:** The practice would benefit markedly from new patients who weren't completely insurance-driven.

3. **Increase monthly new case starts:** The doctors felt that a 50 percent increase, from 24 to 36 per month, would put them in a very good position.

## What SmartBox Did for Drs. O, S, B, and V

Orthodontic treatment is a big financial investment, and the prospects in the doctors' market were looking to minimize that investment by going to lower-price general dentists.

The four orthodontists had vastly more experience and expertise than any general dentist could hope to match. However, the practice marketing wasn't conveying that message well enough. Nor was it tying their experience into reassurance that prospects' investment in orthodontic treatment would be safest by using an expert in the field.

SmartBox reinvented the doctors' marketing approach to help them overcome low-price competitors and get a larger share of traditional orthodontic cases, i.e., braces. Within six months after signing, there was already a noticeable difference in the number of new case starts, and the trend continued upward throughout 2017.

## The Doctors Report

"I couldn't believe it at first," Dr. O said. "I went from having six or seven open appointments a week to being full almost constantly. And that continued month after month. We'd never gotten results like that before from our marketing."

"The best part," said Dr. V, "is that I'm not really having to sell my case solutions much at all. Sure, patients have questions, and I take the time to answer them. But starting treatment isn't an adversarial situation with the vast majority of case starts anymore."

Dr. S agrees. "I read in the free report that new patients would come in presold. Damned if that didn't prove to be true, at least in the large majority of cases. I haven't seen anything like it in 20 years of practice."

"Yeah, what they said," added Dr. B. "The bottom line is looking really good, and I'm very optimistic that by the time I'm ready to bow out, we'll be in a very good place. Things have turned around for us, and I'm confident that they'll stay that way."

The four orthodontists have claimed the high ground in their market and look to hold on to it indefinitely.

You can get your FREE copy of "The Ultimate Case Start Solution" by visiting **www.casestartsolution.com**.

---

# Case Study #5
# The Case of the Spoiled Fruit

**Location:** Western U.S.

**Core Market Base (within 5 miles):** > 140,000 people
**Practice:** Multi-office general dentistry practice
**Longevity:** 30 years
**Main Revenue Streams:** Cleanings and exams; restorations; teeth whitening; minor cosmetic dentistry
**Highest Historical Annual Revenue:** $3.9M
**2015 Revenues:** $3.1M
**SmartBox Start Date:** December 2015
**2016 Revenues:** $3.6M
**2017 Revenues:** $4.4M
**Projected 2018 Revenues:** $5.1M
**Competitors:** 16 general dentistry practices; Aspen Dental (2); Kool Smiles

---

It's not always easy for highly experienced dentists to change with the times. Not clinically—experience has shown that if there's a better way to do something, doctors will adopt it—but in terms of marketing a dental practice.

Most dentists hate the marketing side of the business, and the six doctors at this three-office practice on the West coast were no exception. They had nearly 150 years' experience in dentistry between them, and they were reasonably content to enjoy the fruits of their labors after so many years.

Until the fruits began to spoil. The slow but steady upward climb of the three practices began to turn around. Dr. A, originally the sole owner of the business, had moved to half-time clinical practice and had been handling the practice's marketing for the prior four years. It did not go well.

Dr. A put it this way to me. "I don't get what motivates

younger people these days. I know that makes me sound like an old fogey, and maybe I am, but what worked to drive new patient business even 10 years ago doesn't work anymore. We're spending more on our marketing but not getting enough in return."

Several of the other five doctors agreed. (I won't list them all, or we'd have alphabet soup.) One of them said, "2015 wasn't exactly terrible, but it certainly wasn't our best year by any means. And you know, we were all fairly busy, but the average case value was way down. We took a hit."

Another dentist said, "Our practices aren't high-margin. We're more of a high-volume operation. It doesn't take much of a decrease in value to drive down our revenues."

The three practices had staked out their areas over time, with the last office established seven years prior. They'd done well in their market until something happened, and that something was the arrival of three corporate dentistry practices. Aspen Dental opened offices in 2012 and 2014, and Kool Smiles entered the market in 2013.

"We had to cut our prices to stay competitive," said Dr. A. "Then several other general practices moved into the area, and it was an all-out price war. I think we're better off than the single-dentist practices because we have some economies in terms of supplies and administration. But it's been rough."

The doctors signed with SmartBox in December 2015. They listed three goals for their company:

1. **Increase average case value:** To put their practice back on a sound footing, they were after a 20 percent increase.

2. **Increase new patient flow:** Competition had gotten so bad that the three practices could handle a 15 percent increase with their spare capacity.

3. **Reestablish a strong growth trajectory for the practice:** All the doctors knew that at some point, they'd want to retire. Growth was the best way to ensure they would enjoy the quality of retirement that they felt they'd earned.

## What SmartBox Did for the Doctors

We performed a competitor analysis of the market and discovered that the doctors had become somewhat complacent about modernizing the appearance of their practices. Since the three locations offered the same services as the corporate practices, the lack of a modern and comfortable waiting room and up-to-date operatories were costing them patients.

A demographic analysis showed that there was an affluent market segment. Low-price advertising doesn't appeal to these prospects; they're more focused on the relationship with their chosen doctor and the experience they can expect in the practice.

The doctors agreed to invest in updating the three practices to present a modern and somewhat more upscale appearance. A number of patient comfort options were added. SmartBox worked with local media to ensure that the public was aware of the improvements.

When the remodeling was largely complete, Smart-Box focused on taking the doctors out of the "just another dentist" category. The company's new website and social media positioned the three locations to appeal to the more upscale segment of their market. At the same time, the practices' marketing emphasized dental insurance acceptance and payment plans. This two-pronged approach met the doctors' goals—more patients to keep their chairs full, and better patients to increase the average case value.

And the strong growth trajectory?

### The Doctors Report

"SmartBox's approach to getting new patients is very different than what I'm used to," said Dr. A. "Our marketing was focused on getting patients in chairs this month or next month. SmartBox has built our new patient numbers over time. We're seeing steady increases in appointments month after month. And we're making a lot more money. The growth in revenue is just remarkable."

# Five Different Practices, Uniform Success

Snapshots, even ones as detailed in the case studies, tell only part of the story. What you don't read here is how the mood of the staff improved, how much more often laughter was heard within the practices, and how much the patients appreciated their experiences with the doctors and staff.

Financial success can breed success on many levels. SmartBox is proud to help dentists realize financial success, but it's extremely gratifying to realize that our efforts help change lives.

> The fact that we're getting 70 new people a month that are still willing to come and see us on a Mon-

day through Thursday type deal, which I know isn't ideal for most people, means that we're doing something right, and you guys are doing something right because we're driving people to our door who want to come in and will make an adjustment to their schedule to come and see us and make it a priority.

— **Dr. Sean Hanson, Salem, Oregon**

---

# MEANWHILE, BACK AT THE BUNKER ... ADDITIONAL RESOURCES

I've included this section for dentists who are truly serious about their success. This is optional but valuable reading covering a wide array of topics related to the question of how to attract the patients you want and need to grow your practice.

I'd like to thank Howard Farran for his kind permission to repost our conversations.

## 1. Colin and Howard Farran

Howard Farran is the powerhouse behind the Dentaltown publishing empire, and we go back a ways. He was kind enough to have me on his podcast in the fall of 2017, and our conversation certainly covered the dental marketing landscape.

In fact, we might have covered three or four landscapes.

This isn't a short read—both of us like to talk, I'm

afraid—but it's an extremely valuable one. Don't be put off by the length; there are numerous other useful resources after this transcript.

If you'd rather watch the episode, you'll find it online here:
**https://www.youtube.com/watch?v=mWNLqtRXqkg**

## 770 Market Like a Pro with Colin Receveur: Dentistry Uncensored with Howard Farran

**Howard Farran:** It is just a huge, huge honor for me to bring back, I guess, on the show—I've hardly ever brought a guest back—Colin Receveur is the CEO of SmartBox, a company that helps dentists thrive.

Colin built his first marketing system for his dad in 1997, who's been in private practice since 1981. Colin is in his 20th year helping dentists thrive, he heads up SmartBox, the fastest growing patient attraction firm in the country with 80 full-time employees, growing 100 percent year over year.

I'm a big fan of your podcast, The Patient Attraction Podcast, and you got a lot of views on Dentaltown. I know most people tell me they find the podcast on the Dentaltown app but then they usually subscribe to it on iTunes; you've got a gazillion views just on the Dentaltown app. Tell us about The Patient Attraction Podcast, and thank you so much for doing that podcast to help dentists and for putting it on the Dentaltown app.

**Colin:** Thanks to you for providing a great platform.

It's awesome how you brought all these dentists from around the world together in one big community to collaborate and really grow the profession. The Patient Attraction Podcast was something that I started. I started with a little GoPro camera up in the corner of my car as I drove down the road. Now, we're up to 1,100 something episodes and it's all about—

**Howard:** We have 552 on Dentaltown, you got to update them.

**Colin:** Well, we didn't start putting them on Dentaltown till we were halfway through.

**Howard:** Okay, so you got the last 552 on.

**Colin:** Yeah, we got the most recent on there. It's all about attracting more and better patients. I don't know any dentist that ever said, "I've got enough patients. I'm good to go, I'm set." Everybody wants to grow their practice, everybody wants to maybe not get more patients but maybe grow their case size a little bit and work a little bit less and make the same money. Those are the kind of doctors that we help.

**Howard:** You just pointed out, though, the entire flaw of what you're doing: Why are there no dentists that filled up their practice and can't take any more new patients? If your hygienist can only clean eight people a day and you only got one or two and you've been in that small town of 5,000 in Indiana for 30, 40 years, why do you still need more customers?

**Colin:** Well, your old customers are, unfortunately, expiring. You always have people moving out of the area. If you're not bringing new infusion into the practice, every practice I've ever seen is going to dwindle eventually if you're not looking for that new infusion of new patients.

**Howard:** What do you think the average flip is in a community? Are you in a suburb of Indianapolis?

**Colin:** We're in a suburb of Louisville, Kentucky. We're on the Indiana side of Louisville, Kentucky. Indy is about two hours north of me.

**Howard:** You're in Floyds Knobs?

**Colin:** Floyds Knobs, yeah.

**Howard:** Isn't Woody Oakes around there too?

**Colin:** I could throw a rock and hit Woody's house.

**Howard:** Oh my God, tell him I said hi. He's a great guy. Do you think that advertising dollars should be split 50-50 with more loyalty programs of keeping these new patients for life? Do you think dentists should just always focus on getting more new clients? It seems like the Fortune 500 always talks about loyalty programs and then small businesses always talk about new patients.

**Colin:** If you had to spend 50 percent of your ad dollars on loyalty, you've got a loyalty problem. That being said, any thriving practice should see 50 percent of their new patients coming from referrals, but you shouldn't have to spend 50 percent of your ad dollars to get that. You should spend 10 or 20 percent of your ad dollars on loyalty programs. That's why advertising is so expensive, they have no loyalty. You have to build that trust and build that rapport with your cold prospects, cold leads to get them to call you.

**Howard:** By the way, when we release this podcast, I actually want to release the first one here, that you were show number 69, you know why 69 is my favorite number?

**Colin:** I bet you're about to tell me.

**Howard:** That was how old Mother Teresa was when she got the Nobel Prize. I grew up in Catholic grammar school, high school, Catholic grading and my favorite nun was Mother Teresa and my favorite priest was Martin Luther. That woman was an amazing woman, but it's the perfect joke. A joke, you always have a setup, so you're leaning one way and then you come back with Mother Teresa in Calcutta, so my gosh, anybody that thought I was going the other way, now they got to look at Mother Teresa and say, "What the hell was I thinking?"

Anyway, I love that podcast. I want anybody listening to this—when you go back and listen to that one, but that was two years ago at Townie Meeting. I brought you back on the show because everybody wants to know about marketing, marketing, marketing. So what's changed in the last two years since that podcast? What can you tell my homies today that you didn't know two years ago?

**Colin:** Well, I think it's much like getting a driver's license. The car's changed, the model's changed, there's something newer and greater and flashier out there, but just because the new model comes out doesn't mean you have to go get a new driver's license. If you follow best practices today and you followed best practices two years ago, your marketing is still going to be successful. Now, there's new shiny objects out there, there's new tactics and strategies, but the best practices haven't changed. Does that make sense?

**Howard:** Yeah. What are the best practices? I see one thing, like millennials—they're all going to build their practice on Facebook; the old guys, it's all going to be direct mail. Who's smarter—the old guys like me, the old, fat, senile grandpas doing direct mail like me, or these young kids doing it all on the internet and Facebook and social media?

**Colin:** You can kill it either way, and I think the most successful kinds are doing both. I think it's shortsighted to do one or the other. Direct mail, in most markets, still is very effective, Facebook in those markets is very effective. Why limit yourself to one or the other? Do both and dominate your market.

**Howard:** I would think it would have to have different customers showing up because I just can't see all these grandmas that need implants on their dentures on Facebook, but I see them all walking out every morning and getting their mail and picking up the newspaper on their driveway. Then I hear all the millennials tell me that all the newspapers are dead and all the mailboxes are gone and no one does direct mail and that it all gets thrown away. What's the only thing that you've seen die since you've been in dentistry 20 years? Is the phone book dead, or is the phone book still alive?

**Colin:** I wouldn't say the phone book is dead, I would definitely say it's on life support. I've got maybe one or two clients that still do the phone book, and they're in very, very rural market areas, and they still do well with it. They can spend a thousand or two a month and they can get patients in a $75 range. That being said, yeah, it's definitely on life support. Any reasonable market size and above, it died several years ago. It is no more.

**Howard:** What about newspaper ads?

**Colin:** Newspaper ads can still be effective. The circulation's down on a lot of newspapers, but the biggest thing, I think, is not so much around the medium—the newspaper or magazine or whatever it is—the biggest problem I see is with the approach of marketing. You've listened to some of my podcasts, I refer to the Golden Ages of Dentistry. You remember the days of the '80s and '90s. Like my dad, the dentist opened up shop, he hung up his shingle outside, and that was all the marketing they did. He had floods of new patients coming in just from a sign on the door. Then there was the age of the Yellow Pages, so that was like the easiest entry point. You had to stick your sign on the wall, then you had the Yellow Pages, which was the next easiest point.

That was the directory for everybody, and you paid your dues and you got in the Yellow Pages and you were good to go. Since then, marketing has become complex. There's no one place that you send a check to and you get your advertising anymore. It was easy for so many years in marketing, and now, it's more complex: competition, bidding, and auctioning and all these complex marketing strategies.

The biggest thing with it is not necessarily where you market, but don't think of marketing as a single step. Don't think of, "Okay, I do advertisement and then I get new patients out of it." Think of it as a nurturing process where you get seen and you build trust, maybe they request some information from you, maybe they'd come in for a consult and then you're nurturing them down this path.

Google—many places have released that people are referencing 10, 11, 12 sources of information before they make that buying decision. That's what's fundamentally changed with people. Twenty years ago, people referenced two sources of information, they only had two. Susie, their friend that likes Dr. Farran, and the Yellow Pages of Dr. Farran's ad, and that was it. From there, they have to call your office. Now, there's online reviews and videos and websites and all this stuff, and you have to think of it more as a path rather than an event. It's a process.

**Howard:** I've been reading a lot about your website, Practice Under Siege with The Four Horsemen of Dentistry. When did this come along, and what are your thoughts on the Four Horsemen of Dentistry at practiceundersiege.com?

**Colin:** I think there's four big threats that dentistry is facing right now. Of course, there's corporate dentistry and many markets. You've got your Aspens and Clear-Choices coming in, and they're the big gorilla in the room. They are coming in, they're driving up marketing expenses, and of course they've got economies of scale. They get everything cheaper, they buy lab supplies cheaper, they have more marketing dollars.

You've got more dental grads than ever. You've got dental schools opening up everywhere. You've got older doctors that are extending their retirement because of the Great Recession. You've got more competition.

Insurance sure isn't something to write home about these days. I saw an interesting article, I put it on my blog earlier this week, that four doctors in Massachusetts have filed a class action lawsuit against Delta for what Delta has done in Massachusetts, and I posted it to our Facebook page, talking about how Delta cut their top tier right off.

Massachusetts, and I believe Washington state a couple of years ago—and there's a lot of pushback on that from a lot of guys, a lot of dentists, that that's their livelihood. Then, of course, the economic uncertainty. I'm not standing here with "The End Is Coming" sign, but the fact is, we've been in the largest, the longest bull market since World War II.

To not consider a plan, if there's a small setback in the economy, I think is shortsighted. I'm a big planner, and I think the numbers—it doesn't mean the end is coming tomorrow—but think about what you're going to do and how you're going to prepare for these things in the future is what I push our doctors to do.

**Howard:** I graduated from high school, was a freshman in college in 1980, when out of nowhere, interest rates went to 21 percent. Inflation, unemployment, and interest rates were all double-digit. Then, I graduated from dental school seven years later in '87, in May of '87, and in October, the DOW just nosedived. Then just 2008 was just 10 years ago, so you go from '80 to '87, that's seven years. What's '87 to 2008? Yeah. If you're a young kid coming out of dental school, I just want to tell you that, you never know what's around the corner.

**Colin:** It's just always good to be prepared. Knowing

and preparing for the future, having a reserve and a plan, you can't go wrong. Plan for the worst and hope for the best.

**Howard:** Give my homies a sense of what you're doing. What are they doing? You want them to go to practiceundersiege.com, or do you want them to go to smartboxwebmarketing.com? Your dad, is he still practicing?

**Colin:** He is, since '81.

**Howard:** He's doing a filling and a crown. What's your filling and a crown and a root canal? What are you doing for dentists these days?

**Colin:** Well, Ron isn't doing any fillings or crowns anymore. He's got an associate that does all his GP side. Ron does all surgery, has for the past decade now, so he does anything from single implants all the way up through complex All-on-4s™.

**Howard:** Nice.

**Colin:** That's what he does. All of the marketing systems that we've built are built really around ... Ron is our test bid. Ron is our poster boy for how we build our marketing systems and a sandbox for making sure they work.

If you want to plan and you want to grow your practice, you can find general bread-and-butter patients. You could do new patient mailers and you can grow your practice, you can sign up for all the insurance claims out there. There's nothing wrong with that; there's a lot of great practices that operate under those models.

The doctors that are our best clients are the ones that

want to find a better kind of patient, whether that's an implant patient, Invisalign, cosmetics. Doctors that are looking for that higher-quality patient that, instead of being a thousand or $1,500 or $2,500 average patient value, some of our docs are working in the $10,000 to $20,000 range, like Ron. He works four days a week, does consults two days a week, and does surgeries two days a week. And he's got a thriving practice, even in Floyds Knobs, Indiana, a small suburban market area, suburb of Louisville.

**Howard:** I love the way you say "Louisville."

**Colin:** Yeah. If you say it like you do, we know you're a tourist.

**Howard:** My dad had a Sonic Drive-In in Louisville, Kentucky.

**Colin:** Really?

**Howard:** Yeah, he was a crazy man. The crazy must skip every other generation because I'm normal but all of my four kids are crazy. He had five in the woodshop, he wants to go national, so he went north and put one in Abilene, Kansas, and Kearney, Nebraska. Then he went south and put one is Childress, Texas, then went east and put one in Louisville.

My four years of high school, each summer, I lived in a different city on the new opening, and I loved my summer in Louisville. That was so damn fun, that was so cool.

Childress, Texas, was the most fun because he was gone the whole time and left me in a hotel with his Lincoln Town Car. I was 14 years old, cruising the streets, dragging around in a big old Lincoln Town Car with a hotel. Man, it was just so damn fun.

Most dentists are just going to call you up and say, "Dude, I want more new patients," so when they call you, what do you say?

**Colin:** Well, it's like when a patient calls your office and they say, "Hey. I got this pain, my jaw hurts." What do you tell them?

**Howard:** I need a consultation, we need to talk. I need to meet you, I need to take pictures.

**Colin:** Yeah, you got to do the diagnostics. You got to jump in and do a consult, meet with them, and see what they want. Every practice is different, every market area is different, and figuring out what they need. Sometimes what a dentist calls us and says they want is not necessarily what we establish that they need. Sometimes they're a little bit missing, and connecting those dots is what we do. Putting together a blueprint on our Discovery Call of, Where do these wants and needs align, and how does this plan look? What kind of results do we see is realistic for you to achieve?

**Howard:** I also, really, think it matters on what type of dentistry he wants to do. Invisalign, I think it'd be a totally different patient than needing an implant. Would you agree that the majority of the implant people are elderly?

**Colin:** They're all the members. That's where the money is, that's where your largest edentulous population is, is with your boomers. That generation didn't have access to dental care, they didn't have, in many cases, fluoridated water, which I've heard you talk about at length.

**Howard:** I'm actually on the towel about that now. I think I'm just going to give it up. No, I really am. I think that, as a businessman, you want to listen to your customers, and a couple of us dentists got it in the water here in Phoenix in 1989, and one-fourth was looney tunes, and then it expired in 20 years, and we just had to do it again. They had the big old city council and all that stuff, and the looney tunes are growing, and they hate the government, they think it's a conspiracy.

They don't trust the CDC, they think it's all corruption, bribery, whatever. But my boys keep showing me the comments that people are putting on my Facebook or YouTube. They say, "Dad, there are violent nuts out there, and they seriously believe that you're doing bad things."

It's almost like, "You know what? If the quarter of the people don't want it in the water and you just want to come in to the dental office with twice as many cavities, knock yourself out." Then when they do come in, you say, "Hey, you want this filling to last 40 years? I'll put in silver." "Hell, no, I want the plastic cheap one that lasts six and a half," and I'm like, "Great. You don't want fluoride in the water, you want fillings that only lasts six and a half years? Knock yourself out. I'm here to serve you."

**Colin:** Yup, they don't get it. The—

**Howard:** I don't know if I'm getting tired or given up or just being a businessman. In fact, I think the biggest underserved market right now is the natural toothpaste. Bob Ibsen started that Rembrandt toothpaste, and then Colgate or Crest—I forgot, one of the big boys—has a natural Uncle Tom's, but they don't even know their own market. Basically, there's 20 ingredients on the side of that box.

And these anti-fluoridationists, they have some rules. There's more than five things in that toothpaste and they don't know what every one of them is, they think it's a toxic chemical soup.

Yeah, the edentulous. If you're 64 years old in America, 10 percent have no teeth times two—20 percent are missing half. By 74, in America, 20 percent have zero teeth times two—40 percent are missing half. You're saying the implant market is the boomers, and is the Invisalign market the millennials? Is that a completely different campaign than for implants for you? Is it a completely different target market?

**Colin:** Well, the target market's different, but the mechanism, the strategy, to get people to buy a $5,000 Invisalign case or a $25,000 implant case is still the same. As the transaction increases, so does trust required. And building that trust, whether you're building it with a millennial or with a boomer, it's all the same. People do business with a dentist they know, like, and trust. Never, I would guess, in your career, Dr. Farran, have you ever treated a patient that did not trust you and did not like you?

**Howard:** Are you talking about my ex-wife?

**Colin:** Well, maybe we'll make one exception there, but people go to who they like. They're not going accept treatment if they don't trust what you're telling them. Build trust, build trust.

**Howard:** I think it's another interesting thing, I think

self-limiting beliefs are amazing. I just read the other day that the average price of a new car in the United States is $33,000, and what percent of Americans in their lifetime do you think will buy one new car around that medium price of $33,000?

**Colin:** 40 percent.

**Howard:** Okay, 40 percent, and what percent of dentists have never done one single full-mouth rehab case over $25,000 in their entire life?

**Colin:** Probably 90 percent.

**Howard:** Yeah, and how many has your dad done?

**Colin:** He does three or four a week.

**Howard:** I know, and ClearChoice that you mentioned earlier, they did 18,000 arches last year at $25,000 an arch, $50,000 for a full-mouth, and these dentists, they've never even presented a new car. They've never even had someone come in and say, "For $25,000, we can take everything out and make everything brand-spanking new. You'll drive out of here eating on a Lexus." How do you deal with that roadblock?

When you're looking at marketing costs, if you're on *Shark Tank*, I know the first question Mark Cuban would ask you is, "What is the acquisition cost of a new patient?" And then when you told him, and I ask that to you, and then you told him, you'd say, "What is your average new patient spend?" Delta is saying that for the United States of America, that new patient is $418, and there are guys like your dad whose average new patient spend is several thousand.

**Colin:** The numbers we work from—a solid 800,000-

and-up practice with, of course, good systems in the back end. Average patient value is between $1,200 and $1,800. The average cost that we see to acquire a new patient ranges anywhere from $59 to $91.

**Howard:** How are you keeping all these acquisition costs under $100 a head? A lot of people, when they start doing Facebook ads and banner ads and direct mail campaigns, their acquisition costs is well north of $150, sometimes $300 a head.

**Colin:** We don't see those kind of costs come in until you start getting into the more niched territory. It's not an uncommon for Ron to spend 600 to 900 bucks on a new patient. The average cost, the average value of that patient, is going to start at three grand for a single tooth, an abutment and crown. You spend $600 and get $3,000 back, that's acceptable. You spend $600, $800, $900 on a patient and you get a $10,000 case in the door, now you're rocking and rolling.

And it's lower volume, but if you've got the marketing systems in place and you have the back-end sale systems ... I think that biggest overlooked part is you can't just throw an advertisement out that says you do implants and all of a sudden, all the patients that want implants are going to call your practice. This is, again, is high trust, high reputation.

Patients have to trust you and they have to know that you're their guy. You got an attorney, you got a plumber, you got an electrician—they're your guy. They trust you and you trust them. When you have a leak, when something breaks, you call them, and when you develop that kind of rapport with your patients or prospective patients, your community, you're the implant guy.

You're who they call when they got a problem like that.

**Howard:** What do my homies find if they go to practiceundersiege.com? You got a new book out.

**Colin:** New book, new book, and before everybody bounces off the video here, I'm not even selling it. I'm giving it away. It's *The Four Horsemen of Dentistry: Survival Strategies for the Practice Under Siege.* What it goes back to is the four forces that I've talked about: corporate, competition, insurance reimbursements, and economic uncertainty. And how to overcome each of those four forces to have a thriving practice.

**Howard:** They go to that website, enter your first name and your email, and then what, you email them the book?

**Colin:** We email them a copy of the book, or for $2, we'll send you a hardback edition of the book as well.

**Howard:** All right, well, how do I give you $2 right now?

**Colin:** You opt in right there and it'll take your money.

**Howard:** Nice. What is it on, PayPal?

**Colin:** It's just through a credit card account; pop in your credit card number, $2 for the book, free shipping and handling, and we'll mail you a book. I'll even sign it for you, Dr. Farran.

**Howard:** Nice, nice. A picture of you and your dad, I'd love that. You should post that on Dentaltown.

**Colin:** I'll do just that.

**Howard:** Say, "Howard wanted to see a selfie of you

and your dad." I've heard so much about him, but I don't have a face to put behind that sound.

What are they going to learn in that book? What are they going to do? Should they go to practiceundersiege.com or should they go to smartboxwebmarketing.com?

**Colin:** SmartBox is our website for our work that we do with dentists. If you're interested in seeing how to attract more and better patients in your practice, go to the SmartBox site. If you just want to get the book, you want to read it and digest it on your own time and see what we're talking about, see the kind of strategies that we implement, go to practiceundersiege.com. Two bucks, we'll send you a copy of the book with free shipping and handling. You can see all about what we do and how we do it.

**Howard:** I love your tagline on here. By the way, that video, I like that YouTube video on SmartBox Web Marketing. Do you want us to add that at the end, that YouTube video, at the end of this podcast?

**Colin:** Yeah, we'd love it. That'd be great.

**Howard:** Yeah. Can you do that, Ry? Yeah, you put a lot of work into that video, and that was good. I also love that underneath that video where you say, "Attract more patients in the next six months than in the past six years." How many times can you do that?

**Colin:** Well, there might be a little bit of hyperbole in the topic. That's actually my old book that I released in 2014, but I see so many dentists that have never marketed at all. The 50- or 60-year-old docs, they got 20 good years left in them to practice, and they've never spent a dime on marketing, or their marketing is just not producing. Those are the guys, when you talk about more patients in the next six months than in the past six years, those are the guys that really have huge, huge opportunity to explode within their market area.

**Howard:** What do you think the conversion rate is of the average dental office? I see a lot of dentists doing ads or Facebook ads or doing something to get you to their website, and then when you land on their website, it's like, "Dude, did you buy this at a convention 10 years ago?" What percent of the websites would you consider are lame, and what is the conversion rate of the lame websites versus the hottest website you could build?

**Colin:** I'd say 90 percent of the sites I look at are awful. It's like the old expression, you can't polish the turd. You could have a turdable website and you could spend $10,000 a month on pay-per-click and SEO and whatever you want to do to it, and it's still going to be a turd. What we do with dentists is help them look at the marketing, the advertising, the website, the follow-up, the phone tracking, it's all the system.

It's moving these patients through this system, holding the staff accountable at the other end of the system. We're the only patient attraction firm in the country that handles everything from advertising and marketing all the way through actually scheduling butts in the chairs for our doctors and making sure that the front desk is held accountable to actually scheduling a reasonable percentage of the calls that we generate for them. That's what it really comes down to, is—

**Howard:** What kind of measurements are you able to

get? Back to the first question, how many people do you think go to the average, lame, put-lipstick-on-a-pig dental website, and look at that before one calls the office? What do you think that conversion rate is, just website to call on a lame dental website versus the best you've seen?

**Colin:** I think the average five-year-old website that is just as awful as you and I can probably imagine has zero to none conversion rate. If you've got a five- or 10-year-old website that looks like a brochure online and you have a millennial that's out—listen, I'm a millennial generation.

**Howard:** How old are you?

**Colin:** 33.

**Howard:** What year were you born?

**Colin:** '84.

**Howard:** The first millennials were what, 1980?

**Colin:** The first what?

**Howard:** Millennials start at 1980 and you were born in '84?

**Colin:** I believe so, yeah.

**Howard:** Go ahead, what do you think that conversion rate is on that website you're describing?

**Colin:** Nothing. When I go to a website that looks horrible, I don't even call them, I click back.

**Howard:** Do you think it's 10 to 1, 20 to 1, 100 to 1? You can't say zero in this math equation, you've got to have one. How many would have to hit that website before one would convert?

**Colin:** I think it's a divide-by-zero proposition. I think—

**Howard:** I know, but you can't do that one. I'm throwing that excuse out.

**Colin:** All right, let me back into this number that you're going to hold me to. If a junk website spent $5,000 a month on marketing, I would say that even a poor-performing website that spent $5,000 on marketing it would get five new patients a month.

**Howard:** But how many would land on that site from the marketing to get that five?

**Colin:** I think that's an impossible number to reach because a bad website may not even rank. A bad website might not have enough SEO juice to even rank. That might be why you only got five people to it.

**Howard:** I know, that's why I always say I would never go into your space. I would never go into that business, dental advertising, because you can do the best dental advertising in the world for them, and their website is a dog, and then when they call the office, half the incoming calls go to voicemail, and if a human does answer the phone, they say, "Can you please hold?" Then they blame it on you. It's like, "Dude, we sent 100 people to your website, and only three converted, and two out of three went to voicemail that you'd never even listened to the voicemail or called them back. Then you're saying it's all me."

**Colin:** That's why we don't talk about hits and clicks and conversion rates. Here at SmartBox, we've got a whole team of people that listen to every phone call that comes into the practice.

**Howard:** I just heard the phone call come in.

**Colin:** There you go, that was it. Every phone call that comes in to a practice we're working with, we have a team of ladies that actually listens to the calls and monitors them in real-time, so that our recording is this at the end of the month. You spent this much on this marketing campaign, you got this many phone calls, you didn't answer this many of your phone calls, and from that, you scheduled or didn't schedule this many new patients.

If you spent $5,000 and you answered 60 percent of your phone calls—which the average practice is only answering a little bit over a half of their phone calls during business hours, it's abysmal—then they only schedule half of that, and you have a 20 percent no-show rate of 100 new patients that you generated, you're down in the 10 to 15 new patient range. So much revenue by way of new patients is lost in the funnel.

They don't answer the calls or they don't schedule them, which is why we give so much attention not only to the marketing and our patient attraction systems to get the phone ring, but an equal amount of attention to making sure these doctors have good front desks, that they answer their calls, that they are appointing the patients at 80 percent or 90 percent. We have a guarantee, and our guarantee is void if the doctor doesn't answer 90 percent of his phone calls.

That's how we help hold the doctors accountable so listen, "We're going to make your phone ring, but if you don't answer your calls, don't come back and yell at us. Listen, here's all these calls you didn't answer. Now, we'll guarantee it if you answer all the calls we send in." We approach it very differently than a lot of marketing agencies, because we're not a marketing agency, we're a patient attraction firm. To attract new patients, you have to take it all the way to the butts in the chairs.

**Howard:** Yeah, I love what you're doing. It's funny, if you left dentistry, everyone else would call your front desk lady. You call her a front desk lady, you name her after a piece of furniture, and she's really almost like a, in any other business, she'd be inbound telemarketing. She would be answering those calls and she's not dialing out, she's not outbound telemarketing dialing for dollars, she's receiving inbound calls for marketing leads. She would be completely trained on how to take that incoming call within three rings and convert it to a schedule to patient.

Then you go in the dental office, and here's the hygienist checking out a patient and says, "Hey, Colin. Why don't you schedule her for a cleaning at six months because you're not doing anything, you're just a receptionist named after a piece of furniture, and can you get me a cup of coffee?" Then the hygienist comes out and says, "I want to buy this new book from Colin Receveur, will you order this for me?"

It's like, "Dude, the phone's ringing. She's inbound telemarketing and she's making you coffee and scheduling." I tell the hygienists to schedule their own damn patients, the assistant will schedule their crown seats and all that kind of stuff, because when that phone rings, it's going to answer and it's got to roll over to other lines, and I cannot believe that half the phone calls in dental offices, every single day, go to voicemail. Then they blame it on Obama and Trump and North Korea and Putin and the Ukraine. It's like, "Dude, I'm pretty sure it was your office that you owned that didn't answer half the phone calls."

**Colin:** Yup. Of course, we work exclusively with dentists, but I've got a lot of friends that are business owners, I've shown them how we monitor calls, and a lot of them do the same systems in chiropractic and personal training. We've compared stats, and it's amazing how many more calls go unanswered in dentistry than in every other market I've compared to. I think it really comes down to, it's not the dentists' fault—they're wearing seven hats.

They're in the back doing restorative—they don't have time to be upfront and monitoring what Suzie Q is doing. If they're staggering their lunches and how many phone lines and if they're holding people accountable to following the best practices of appointing patients. It's really, I think, a resource issue. Dentists need help, they need to be doing dentistry, that's where they make their money. They don't make money managing and playing around on their website, they make money doing dentistry. That's their most profitable activity.

**Howard:** Nice reference to Suzie Q of the Creedence Clearwater Revival. That was one of the 20 greatest songs of the '70s. God dang, I love that song. Do you remember that song?

**Colin:** I've heard it, I can't say I remember it because that was before my time.

**Howard:** Oh my God, I thought maybe you heard your dad play it in the background. Yeah, so how are you getting metrics? What are measuring and how do you measure it?

**Colin:** We not only track phone calls coming in, but we have a team of people that listen to every call. The metrics at the end of the month are total calls and then how many of these were answered, scheduled, and not scheduled. We know how much marketing was spent on a marketing campaign, whether TV, radio, billboard, internet, whatever it is, and then out the other end, we know how many actual butts were scheduled into the chairs. From that, you divide them and you get a per patient acquisition cost.

**Howard:** How do you actually measure that incoming call? How do you listen to it? What are you using?

**Colin:** We hire a team of people to do it. I get a team of ladies that listen, literally, to every call in near real-time and click-tag that call based on what happened on it.

**Howard:** Now, do you have to have that warning message, "This call may be monitored for ..." Do you have to have that?

**Colin:** In some states. There are some states that require that, there are some states that don't.

**Howard:** What practice management software do you like working with the most to be able to monitor if that patient was scheduled or that kind of stuff?

**Colin:** We work with all of them, Dentrix, Eaglesoft.

**Howard:** Which one do you like working with the

most? If some new millennial was going to start a de novo and get a practice management software, you get to see all the softwares. Is there one that you like more than the other?

**Colin:** I think there are perks. The new software that's developed in the cloud that's really cool. Of course, the advantage is that you don't have to have in-house IT, servers, and such. The downside is, of course, you better make sure your internet works damn well. The phone systems that have come out that pair—have you seen the Weave phone systems?

**Howard:** Yes.

**Colin:** They're pretty cool, where they can integrate in and pull it right up on the screen as the calls come in. I don't work in a PMS, practice management system, myself, I can't say I recommend one over the other anymore than just to talk generally about the pros and cons of them.

**Howard:** Well, back to that VoIP, you got to have a phone system. Most dentists are getting their phone from their cable company or internet, but some of these VoIP, if you go to Dentaltown and do a search— if you switch to a VoIP, a voice-over-internet protocol, now all your phone calls are coming in ones and zeros, you can do a lot of that information.

But some of these dentists are finding out that their internet is not as reliable as they thought they were. It's one thing to think your internet is reliable when you're surfing Dentaltown or Facebook or LinkedIn, but it's a whole 'nother thing when it's your sole incoming phone call. Do you think VoIP, is there enough for your average dentist, or do you think it's just too general of a question and it really depends what city you live in? What is your experience with VoIP?

**Colin:** I come from a techy background, Howard, so I can talk about VoIP and latency and bandwidth all day long. I don't want to get too techy here and destroy everybody's minds with latency of your typical cable modem versus latency of a DSL line or a fiber line.

**Howard:** What does latency even mean?

**Colin:** Latency is how long it takes for the information to travel from your office to the first hub, the first router in that connection. Effectively, what is important to people that are considering VoIP is if they're going to do VoIP, don't run it over your cable, your Spectrum, Comcast cable modems. If you're going to do VoIP, look at DSL, look at fiber. You're going to have to pay a little bit more for your internet access because typically, cable, the latency on your typical cable modem is poor, and you get a lot of that chop, the cutout.

**Howard:** Would you talk about Cox Cable or, what were the other ones you mentioned? The cable companies.

**Colin:** Spectrum, Comcast, Insight, all the big cable providers.

**Howard:** You would say not do VoIP over cable, but you said fiber optic, I understand, but what was the DSL?

**Colin:** DSL and fiber both are going to be a much more solid platform for VoIP if you're going to run it.

**Howard:** Okay. Is fiber optics, obviously, better than

DSL? Is that the gold standard—fiber optic?

**Colin:** It's the new standard. Having a DSL line, a copper-dedicated line, is never going to go away. Every neighborhood in the country has copper lines running through it. Fiber is the new stuff. It's uber reliable, super fast, it really just depends what's in your neighborhood. We run all VoIP-powered, my father runs all VoIP, when we both have fiber lines run into our buildings, so it works really well for us.

**Howard:** Is he using Weave?

**Colin:** He's not, no, but he's looking at it. I pointed him to it. I'm trying to get him on it.

**Howard:** Yeah, yeah. That's kind of a funny thing because you talk about these copper lines laying around—people don't realize that the phone was just the telegraph 2.0 and the internet was just the telegraph 3.0. The telegraph to the phone and the internet, they still ran on the same copper line, and it's all in the same space of communication. I wonder what the fourth line would be; from telegraph to phone to internet, I wonder what's next?

**Colin:** Much faster internet. Fiber is going to be able to bring us up to the standards of the rest of the world. A lot of people think the U.S. has this great internet infrastructure—we are actually poorer among other first-world countries for internet access. There's a lot of good fiber initiatives right now bringing the United States as a whole, providing a lot more connectivity, a lot more underprivileged connectivity, as well as high speed for businesses.

**Howard:** I think the coolest idea that I've heard now,

I think, is going to be the greatest new company is, when you put a satellite up there for internet, it's 25,000 miles up. It takes a few seconds for that message to go up to the satellite and then come back down, and they realize that on any given moment, the world has 27,000 airplanes in the air, and if they put an internet Wi-Fi thing on the belly of those planes, it's like having your internet at 25,000 miles up there on a satellite, it'll only be about 25,000 to 35,000 feet. And this guy I heard, listening to from MIT, said that if they would put that on the bottom of every airplane, almost the entire world would have internet connection tomorrow. Ain't that just crazy?

**Colin:** Well, that's exactly what Mark Zuckerberg is doing in Africa. He has launched, he has that drone solar-powered aircraft that can fly for six months at a time and is providing wireless connectivity for huge swaths of area. These launched in Africa, so yeah, it's an awesome idea. Just on the edge of being implemented, just by limitations of technology right now. That's a great idea. Now, who's going to pay to deploy it, right?

**Howard:** Right. Money is the answer, what's the question?

**Colin:** Yes, exactly. Exactly. Yup.

**Howard:** What else do my homies need to know? Again, you monitor them, how do you monitor that that phone call was answered to being scheduled to a butt in the chair? How do you monitor the phone call answered to showing up on their schedule?

**Colin:** Like a lot of marketing companies do out there, we track the calls and we record the calls. We then have a team of people that go in and—we're a fully HIPAA-compliant company, so we've been through all the same HIPAA training that any dental practice goes through, probably more, because we've had to certify all 80 people in our company.

Our team listens, then, to the recorded calls, and we deliver a report at the end of the month to the doctor that says, "Hey, here's this marketing campaign A, B, and C. Here's how many calls scheduled and not scheduled and not answered calls came from it."

**Howard:** With these 80 people, you're putting your people physically in the office? These are people around the country or this is all done digitally?

**Colin:** Digitally, it's all in the cloud. Our Zetetics call system is in the cloud, we track and record the calls for all of our practices around the world. Then, my team here in New Albany, Indiana, logs in to the cloud and listens to them and tags them based on what happened on that call.

**Howard:** Dude, how old did you say you were? How old are you? Thirty-three?

**Colin:** Thirty-three.

**Howard:** Thirty-three to have 80 employees. Dude, you are crushing it.

**Colin:** Well, thank you. It's been a long road, and I had some good advice along the way from my dad and others.

**Howard:** You know how many people work for me?

**Colin:** How many?

**Howard:** About half. That's what I always tell them as they punch me in the rib. No, seriously, that is amazing. Where's your company headed? What's next for you?

**Colin:** Well, we want to help 10,000 dentists by 2020. To get there, we're launching some additional products that are going to help dentists in addition to our marketing and our call platform. We've got a few new products that I'm not going to reveal just yet, that are coming online later this year that are going to be instrumental to really spread our wings out and be able to help dentists grow, to thrive, to attract more and better patients, which is our motto. It's not just volume, but the guys we work with, the private practice dentists, are wanting to not go to the insurance route. They've been fee-for-service for their whole livelihood, and that's how they want to finish.

**Howard:** Well, America doesn't realize it, but the whole planet, seven and a half billion people, they got the same brain, they have the same needs, wants, desires, and they're all in different stages of their dental journey. I think the United States is following the NHS about 20 years. When I got out of school 30 years ago, everybody worked for the NHS, but the fees just kept going lower and lower and lower, and finally dentists had to go bankrupt or they said, "Okay, I can't do this fee schedule anymore."

Now, there are dentists, there's like 5,000, that are totally out of it, and since your dad and I got out of dental school, the fees from dental insurance companies have been reduced about 42 percent for the country, and 10 years from now, it'll be 50, 60, 70 percent reduction.

They're all eventually going to have to have their fees lowered to where they can't do dentistry they do on their kids on this insurance scheme.

Then they're going to have to realize that the people in New Albany, Indiana, are going to have to pay for their implants the same way they pay for their iPhone and their car and their house and their trip to Disneyland. They just have to get out their wallet and pay for it, and I think it's a journey that dentists don't want to hear. They want to hear that the insurance is going to get better, they want to call the PPO and try and negotiate to raise their fee, and they're trying to go back in time. I just think there's too many examples in other countries, especially the United Kingdom, of how this road is going to play out.

**Colin:** Like you said, the reimbursements haven't gone up in 30 years. Discretionary spending on dentistry, as a whole, has not increased since 2008. While the population has increased, spending has remained flat in the last decade. With corporate coming in, with these new grads coming out of school, that corporate can hire them for fractions of what it costs to hire a dentist a decade or 20 years ago. A lot of states are introducing that mid-level dentist, not the dentist, but like the nurse practitioner of dentists.

**Howard:** Georgia just signed that bill yesterday, that a hygienist can work independently in a whole list of situations.

**Colin:** The direction that the industry is going is towards cheaper and lower reimbursements, and if you pursue that 60 percent of the population that is looking for cheap and fast, that's who you're going to get.

You're going to get the industry as a whole. There are still a lot of people out there that want somebody they know, like, and trust, that are willing to look outside their insurance network and pay for it, and if you can build trust and you can be their guy, there's still lots of dentistry out there to be done.

It's just like the medical industry. Here in New Albany, in Louisville, the big medical change, Floyd Memorial in our area, Baptist, have all bought up all the independent practitioners. Yet, there's still private practitioners that are practicing around the area, and there'll always will be. I think dentistry is a decade behind medicine. I think if you want to see where dentistry is going to be in a decade, look where medicine is right now—the insurance companies rule the roost, they dictate everything that goes on—that's where you're going to see dentistry at in a decade. If you don't like that paradigm, start preparing, start changing your model now. Ron started his implant transition in '05, '06, '07.

**Howard:** That's your dad?

**Colin:** That's my dad, yeah.

**Howard:** You call your dad Ron?

**Colin:** Yeah, I do it. Everybody makes fun of me, but we have so many business interactions that I've just always called him Ron. It took him five years, of course, it was in the middle of the recession, but five years later, he had this implant thing really cranking. When he's doing $3.5, $4 million a year in implants right now, working three days a week, it's pretty incredible.

He had a guy fly in last month from the Caribbean to

do an All-on-4 on him. He's pulling in people from, not even just regionally, but internationally, as we can now say it legitimately, to do implant work. That kind of presence you don't grow in 12 months. Twelve months in his implant kit, he had a solid implant practice. As I talk, it's walking patients down this path, building trust, nurturing them, and showing them you're really here to help them. They can trust you. Building that trust up is paramount for dentists.

**Howard:** When I got out of school in '87, only rich people could fly on Braniff and Delta. Really, the planes were only a third full, and everybody was pretty much wearing a suit and tie or a dress and shoes. Southwest has made flying so low cost that these dentists that are getting people to come up from the Caribbean—they got to get a dental camera, and they got to start photo-documenting their work, because those people want to see your work on the website.

You and I both agree that 90 percent of the dental websites are a polished turd, and you have to nail dental photography and you have to put "This is all my work from Ron" on that website.

What's really bizarre is there are patients who think, "Well, you're not going to get the best dentistry in Salina, Kansas, so I'm shopping around these really high-falutin dentists in Kansas City, and I'm going to fly up to Kansas City and have it all done there."

Then that dentist there finds out what town she's from, and she isn't aware that there's some guy with a Diplomat of the International Congress of Oral Implantology that he's met several times at classes, and it's all because that guy was all that, but nobody would know it by going to his website.

**Colin:** That's it. Yup, that's all too common.

**Howard:** Also from that 2008 crash, the American Dental Association actually hired one of the greatest health care economists that have ever lived in the last 10, 20 years, and I love his last blog. Dentists, lawyers, and lattes—those were the only three industries that have not recovered to their pre-2008 levels. After that crash, so many people said, "You know what? I can't buy a Starbucks every morning for $5. Five dollars times 365 days a year is one area I can cut back." What is that, 365 times five? Shit, that's $1,800 a year, and a lot of these lawyers, these sites—what are those do-it-yourself lawyer websites where you just buy all the standard forms for ... ?

**Colin:** Prepaid legal, yeah.

**Howard:** What is it called, paid legal?

**Colin:** Prepaid legal is the one I've seen.

**Howard:** Yeah, prepaid legal and lattes and dentists in the minds of a lot of people has turned into a commodity. Isn't it filling a filling a filling?

**Colin:** Isn't it? Yeah. A crown is a crown is a crown. How many $400 crowns do you have in your mouth?

**Howard:** Seven. I have seven gold onlays. My friends put them in, and I didn't even have to pay to have them filled, so ...

**Colin:** The consumers don't know the difference, a $500 crown versus a $1,000 crown versus a $1,200 or $1,500 crown. You're right, things are commoditized to the point that that is the 60 percent of consumers that are fueling corporate dentistry right now. The part that they want the cheapest price, they want the best hours, and they just want to show up and get it done, and they don't care if they have a relationship with their dentist. The same way with medicine. How many people go to only outpatient clinics or emergency cares these days versus actually have a doctor that they know by name?

A much, much larger percentage, exponentially larger than there were 20 years ago. That's the direction the industry is going, is cheaper care like Georgia did, they introduced the intermediate dentists. That's what consumers are speaking with their wallets, and a lot of times, I talk to dentists and they say, "Well, it's the insurance companies, and the ADA is screwing us," and all these. It is them, but I think they're missing the bigger picture: that the consumers, at large, are voting with their pocketbooks, and this is the vote that people are casting. If it wasn't, there wouldn't be any fuel for these machines that are being built.

**Howard:** Yeah, it's funny. They always blame it on everything but themselves. I'm a big proponent of your website has to have a YouTube video of your chemistry. There are so many adorable, amazing dentists who just don't come off well on a photograph, but if you click into the YouTube video and you're going to see this guy is warm and fuzzy and nice and you trust them and all that kind of stuff, they don't know that 10 people had to go to their website before one call. They don't realize that half the calls weren't answered.

Then, so their entire practice works in this little middle of the funnel where there'll bring in $6.75 and take home a $1.45, and then they don't realize that by the time they got 5,000 charts, 4,000 are gone because the hygienist cleaned eight people today but she only scheduled six for a recall.

Then in six months, one of them called and said, "I can't come in today, I'll call you back tomorrow"—no one ever called her back, and they just keep falling off. All these little ... just falling off, and then the dentist is having high staff turnover. It seems like all the million-dollar practices I know, the average staff has been there about seven years or more, and there are so many of these corporate chains where they can't even keep the dentist there for 20 months. Then they hire a new dentist, they found out that the assistant just got a job there yesterday.

**Colin:** Yeah, yeah. I got a friend that graduated from UofL School of Dentistry a couple of years ago, and he went to work at a corporate chain. It was him and another dentist, and they would strategize, and they would play against each other for who was going to do the hygiene check and who was going to get that patient waiting in the waiting room. They'd had quotas to meet, and the doctor that got the waiting room patient got more towards his quota than the hygiene check. Patient care was shit because you had two dentists that were eyeing to fill their quota faster, because a non-dentist—a businessperson, not a dentist—is assigning them quotas for how much care they had to present and close.

**Howard:** I know, and it's sad. Some of these offices, if a patient has a five millimeter pocket or greater, you got to put in these minocycline chips. These are medical decisions made by nonmedical people, and my question is, in medicine, if all the physicians and dentists work for the insurance company, then where do the Americans go if they need a doctor?

**Colin:** Good question, we'll find out in a decade.

**Howard:** The answer to corporate dentistry is personal dentistry. That's what I would do. I would sit there where you're following the UK, the fees are going to get lower and lower and lower, the volumes will get so high, the fee is so low. Eventually you'll say, "Hell, I can't send my children to this office." So eventually, you'll start and say, "Well, instead of a corporate care, low-fee, high-volume, I'm going to do personal care, low-volume, high-fee," and if you want it done once and right, it's usually cheaper in the end run anyway.

**Colin:** The biggest private medical clinic here in Louisville, Kentucky, is a subscription clinic. For the privilege of joining their clinic, their practice, you pay $10,000 a year, and that's just to have one physical a year done. You still pay for all of your other visits. If you want direct access to the doctor, you'll literally get his cell phone number, you can call him 24 hours a day, $10,000 a year for a family of four gets you access into that, and then they still bill you at the regular rate.

It's an interesting model with medicine, because like I said, I think medicine is where dentistry will be in 10 years, right now. I think you're going to see more of these in-house finance plans that you've seen everywhere, I think this subscription model is something that we'll see play out in dentistry. I don't really have a clear bearing yet on it, but it's a very successful model that I've seen here in Louisville and other areas in these. It'll be cool to see where it goes in the next decade.

**Howard:** Yeah, and there will always be price segmentation of any market, going from a Cadillac to a Pontiac, to Olds to Buick to Chevy. When you go to these countries that socialize medicine, half the country just loves it because everything is free. If you wanted the high-end, it's not necessarily delivering, with the exception of the country of Taiwan.

Hey, that was the fastest hour ever. Big fan of your work. I actually watched our first podcast before you came back on today because hell, that was just as informative. That was amazing.

**Colin:** Live at the Townie Meeting, didn't we, in Vegas?

**Howard:** Yeah, we did. We did. That was an awesome time, and now, the next two years, it's going to be in Orlando.

**Colin:** I'm looking forward to it, I hope to be there.

**Howard:** Well, we always go to Vegas, but there's a difference in boomers and millennials. Millennials aren't into going into a casino and smoking and gambling and all that Rat Pack stuff of yesteryear. They're more into Orlando, and I got grandkids now, and my grandkids want to go see Mickey and Minnie and Goofy and Pluto. I'm so good I even know that—you know how to tell the difference between Goofy and Pluto?

**Colin:** One is orange is one's not.

**Howard:** Goofy is the one with the big goofy teeth; the other one don't show his teeth.

**Colin:** There you go.

**Howard:** See, a dentist would only notice that. You noticed the color, I noticed that Goofy has two goofy-looking teeth, and the other one ain't showing any teeth.

**Colin:** I got three kids under four, and we're doing our first Disney trip next year. I probably ought to figure that kind of stuff out.

**Howard:** All right, well, go Goofy. Seriously, man, thanks. How many posts you have on Dentaltown? You've answered so many posts, you've uploaded 500 podcasts on the Dentaltown and the app. You've done so much for dentistry, you've done so much for Dentaltown. Thank you so much for all that you've done, for dentistry, your dad Ron, and Dentaltown.

**Colin:** Thanks for the opportunity, I appreciate it, doctor.

**Howard:** All right, we'll talk to you later. When you see Woody Oakes, have him come up on my show.

**Colin:** I'll tell him, I'll tell him. Maybe I'll have lunch with him, I'll send him your way.

# 2. Preliminary Steps

You might not be ready to implement your own patient attraction system or to have SmartBox handle the work of getting you a steady stream of new patients.

Fair enough.

I mentioned before that I want all dentists to be successful. From the **SmartBox blog** in August 2017, here are some tips to help you figure out where your current marketing approach is letting you down.

# Track Down the Weaknesses in Your Dental Marketing

Dentists aren't detectives, although some diagnostic puzzles may challenge your deductive skills. But one area where dentists can benefit from doing some investigation is their online marketing.

Dentists aren't trained as marketers. For that reason, many dentists' marketing violates a lot of the rules that determine good marketing. That may or may not be the case with your marketing. Regardless, here are four mistakes dentists make with their marketing that you should avoid at all costs.

### Number 1: Limiting the number of marketing channels

Almost no business needs to be in every marketing channel, but few businesses can do well appealing to their prospects in just one or two channels. Some dentists still ignore the online environment and rely on newspaper ads and postcard campaigns. Today, 90 percent of people who are looking for a dentist begin their search online. At an absolute minimum, you should have a well-written, well-designed, SEO- and mobile-compliant website in addition to offline marketing channels. Depending on the primary demographic you're trying to attract, you might want to add additional channels like Facebook or Instagram.

## Number 2: Having an inconsistent message

Too many dentists have one or more disconnects between parts of their marketing. For instance, they try to position themselves as dental experts who offer extensive discounts and low-price work. That smacks as an insincere come-on to prospects, much like a hotel offering deluxe accommodations for $40 per night. As another example, some dentists focus on patient comfort in one part of their marketing while touting their advanced technology in another part. In yet another channel, they're pushing appointment availability. Your prospects would have to see different ads in different channels to get an overall impression of your practice.

## Number 3: Failing to direct prospects to the website

Research indicates that a dentist's website is the single most influential marketing vehicle for converting prospects into appointed patients. That makes sense, because no other marketing channel can convey in one place the breadth of information available on your site. For that reason, every piece of your marketing, online and off, should include a call to action to visit your website.

## Number 4: Not converting prospects to receive additional information

Google says that people consult an average of 10.4 sources of online information before making a purchasing decision. That figure applies to the purchase of services as well as goods. The vast majority of your prospects aren't ready to immediately commit, so you need to stay in front of them until they're ready to choose you. By offering something of value on your website, such as a white paper or an article that relates to their dental concern, you can obtain prospects' email addresses. That will allow you to send them additional information until they're ready to choose you.

Again, these weaknesses may not apply to your marketing. But if they do, address them and you'll not only attract more new dental patients, you'll increase your marketing return on investment. And what dental practice wouldn't go sleuthing after that?

# 3. Getting Social

Dentists who want to stand out from their competitors would do well to establish a strong social media presence. To give you a really good head start on picking one or more venues, here's a **Patient Attraction Podcast**™ from January 2018.

# The 3 Social Media Platforms Dentists MUST Be On

Patient Attraction Episode 1121

A lot of dentists still believe that all they need to get enough new patients is a great website. That was true at one time, but the online environment has moved on. These days, dentists also need a strong social media presence to stay competitive. Why? Because your competition is catching on to the fact that prospects use social media. But not all social media platforms are created equal. And not all those platforms are worth dentists' time. After the break, I'll tell you how to maximize your return on investment by focusing on just three social media sites. Stay tuned.

Thanks for watching the Patient Attraction Podcast™. I'm Colin Receveur, founder and CEO of SmartBox.

If you're not social media savvy, it can be kind of bewildering. There are thousands of sites with odd names like Facebook, Tumblr, Instagram, Snapchat, and many, many others.

With so many choices, how are you supposed to know which ones your dental prospects are on? Even if you're on social media, it's hard to know where to invest your time and attention.

SmartBox's research and experience shows that there are just three social media platforms worth the effort for dentists. Those three are Facebook, Google+, and Twitter.

Let's start with Facebook, the undisputed king of social media.

Facebook claims to have over two billion users worldwide. There are 200 million users in the U.S. That's nearly 2 out of 3 people in the country. The sheer number of people using Facebook is reason enough to focus on it. The odds are overwhelming that most of the prospects you want to attract have Facebook accounts.

The demographics you want are on Facebook, too. Roughly 53 million users are between the ages of 25 and 34. Thirty-eight million are between 35 and 44. And 32 million are ages 45 to 54.

More women than men are on Facebook, and women are usually the dentistry decision-makers in a household.

Facebook has been limiting the organic reach of posts. Currently, it's below 6 percent and headed downward. But paid Facebook ads offer a host of options for targeting the people you want to reach.

If you were going to focus on only one social media platform, Facebook would be it. But dentists need to look at a wider audience.

Over 90 percent of people today begin their search for a dentist online. Google is still the undisputed king of search with a three-fourths market share. And when people search for a dentist in your market, hopefully they'll find your practice.

Once they do, they'll see your Google+ page.

Your Google+ page is essentially a build-out of your Google My Business page. The sidebar that appears in a search can contain patient reviews about their experiences in your practice. And it serves as a source of additional information for prospects.

Dentists want to carefully consider how they can best use Google+ and make it a vital link in their marketing efforts.

The last vital social media platform for dentists is Twitter. With its current 280-character limit, Twitter is the easiest and fastest way to engage current patients and prospects online.

The demographics of Twitter are in dentists' favor. Thirty-seven percent of Twitter users are between ages 18 and 29, and one-quarter are 30 to 49 years old.

Facebook, Google+, and Twitter are the three most profitable social media platforms for dental practices. However, maintaining a strong social media presence is something almost all dental practices struggle with.

The whole purpose of social media is to create engagement between people, or people and companies. You and your staff are busy, and there's no time for responding promptly to online comments and questions.

SmartBox's full-package dentists only need to handle the day-to-day posting on social media. SmartBox creates and auto-posts a vast amount of original, informative, and helpful content to keep the social media platforms relevant and boost their SEO. Every month, we add professionally written blogs, infographics, videos, quizzes, and more to our doctors' Facebook and Google+ pages.

Maintaining our doctors' social media presence is part of our industry-leading Patient Attraction System™. Discover what our **Patient Attraction System**™ can do for your practice. Visit smartboxdentalmarketing.com and reserve your free Practice Discovery Session™. We'll show you how we can double or even triple your practice.

Join me for our next podcast. Until then, keep moving forward.

# 4. But ... Her Newsletters!

Dental newsletters can still be effective marketing tools, if they're done right.

Unfortunately, very few newsletters these days actually produce new patient appointments. If that's true of your newsletter, or if you're considering starting one, you'll be interested in this article from the September 2017 issue of our **Patient Attraction Magazine**™.

## Make Them Read All About It

Newsletters are still a mainstay of dental marketing these days. Done right, newsletters keep your current patients informed and encourage your prospects to pick up the phone and make an appointment. Done wrong, newsletters wind up being briefly scanned and deleted ... if that.

There are a lot of factors involved in creating a winning dental newsletter, but the two most important are content and timing. Let's take those in order.

**Ready, Fire, Aim?**

Most dentists have a rough idea of what they want to write about, because it's what they want their patients and prospects to know. And dental practices usually have a more-or-less set schedule for releasing newsletters, either because it's convenient or it's all the practice can manage.

Those dentists are spending time, money, and effort without knowing exactly what their audiences want to read. This is almost the definition of bad marketing. However, you don't have to follow in their footsteps. With surprisingly little effort, you can find out what your patients and prospects want to read about and how often they want to read it.

In-office patient surveys are a fast and inexpensive way to get the information you need from your patients. If you have waiting times—even short ones—before appointments, that would be a great time to hand out a short survey. List a variety of topics in plain English and/or other languages, depending on your market's demographics, and make the responses check-the-box.

You can also offer online surveys to capture your patients and your prospects. Depending on the number of responses you want to capture, SurveyMonkey is free for up to 100 responses or $35 a month for up to 1,000 responses. You might consider adding an occasional survey to your website.

The bottom line is that you don't have to fire blindly with your newsletter when you know what to aim at. Learn what your audience wants to read, and your newsletter will be a much more effective marketing tool.

**Don't Be Content with Bad Content**

Now you know what interests your readers. The next step is to produce content worth reading. That's not necessarily as easy as it might sound.

Dental practices are in the business of seeing patients and solving their dental problems. For that reason, many practices treat their newsletters as an afterthought. That's understandable—in a busy dental practice, the additional responsibility of writing and producing a monthly newsletter, or even a quarterly one, can become a burden. As a result, quality can suffer, and quality is absolutely necessary these days if you're going to keep your chairs full. Everything you do, and everything you put out in your marketing, reflects on your practice.

Here are four suggestions for producing great dental newsletter content.

**Number 1: Delegate newsletter creation tasks by your staff's interests and ability.**
One of your staff people may be a good writer, while another may have an artistic bent. Yet another may be an excellent photographer. Delegating different aspects of creating a newsletter lessens the burden, allowing your practice to produce better content on schedule.

**Number 2: Keep it short and readable.**
The newsletter as well as the individual articles should be quick and easy to read. People are more pressed for time than ever, and attention spans are shorter. The equivalent of a four-page online newsletter will do for most practices, while some offices might send out a two-page missive. Regardless, your content should be written at roughly a middle school reading level, which is optimal for online reading. A variety of readability checkers online can help you fine-tune your writing.

**Number 3: Punch it up.**
Tasteful, colorful photos and graphics add to your newsletter's appeal and keep readers interested. Also, add white space between paragraphs to make online scanning easier.

**Number 4: Edit and proofread.**

With online spelling and grammar checkers, there's no reason your newsletter should be riddled with typos and bad grammar. Again, your newsletter reflects you and your practice. Professionals should produce professional marketing materials.

## It's Just a Matter of Time

Your priority should determine the frequency that you send out your newsletter. That should happen just often enough to accomplish your goals. People are swamped by emails and snail mail pieces. Too many communications to your patients and prospects is as bad as too few.

This is another area where surveys can be extremely useful. While there's no frequency that will satisfy everyone, responses will typically cluster around one or two points on a proposed release schedule—monthly, bimonthly, quarterly, or semiannually, for example. If you're automating your newsletter release, and you have opt-in data for your prospects and patients, you can time the release to their preferred schedules.

## Keep the End Goal in Sight

You can use your dental newsletter to stay in contact with your prospects, to humanize your staff to your patients, and to inform your readership of interesting and useful developments … if you do it well.

Above all, your newsletter can serve to help convert prospects to appointed patients, which is the end goal of all your dental marketing.

# 5. Some Things Never Change

I mentioned earlier in this book that the internet continues to evolve at light speed. But for dentists who are determined to do their own marketing, here are some "evergreen" ideas from our **Patient Attraction Podcast**™ about what it takes to be a confident and successful dentist.

I say that these are evergreen points because we're well over 1,000 podcasts now. This is from episode 188, way back in 2014 (an eternity in internet time).

But they're just as true today as they were then.

## 9 Traits of Confident Dentists

Patient Attraction Episode 188

Hey, everyone, Colin Receveur here on this fine Friday, August 8. I'm confident I have something you can use when we return.

Since I began SmartBox Marketing, I've talked with untold numbers of dentists. I've talked with millionaires and I've met guys so far in debt they thought they would never get out.

I've seen successful dentists and I've seen dentists who ultimately failed. I've seen plenty of guys in between.

One thing that stands out to me is that confidence breeds success. So here is a list of my own observations and those of experts in the shared traits of confident dentists:

**1. Confident dentists are more worried about doing what is right than being right.**

This means a confident dentist can give an initial diagnosis or propose a solution and then change his mind or go a different direction. Confidence isn't defending your decisions to the end; confidence is being secure enough to do the right thing even when it wasn't your original plan.

**2. Confident dentists listen more than they speak.**

A confident dentist doesn't have to impress you with what he knows. He wants to know what his patient wants or what his advisor can tell him that he may not know. Confidence is knowing what you know but not having to show it off.

**3. Confident dentists don't have to be the center of attention.**

A confident dentist is happy when others get credit. That may mean a staff member or a patient. A confident dentist doesn't care who gets credit as long as there is a reason for credit to be given.

**4. Confident dentists know they don't know everything.**

Asking for help or information isn't a sign of weakness. It actually shows that the dentist has enough confidence is his other knowledge that he can acknowledge what he doesn't know. This can be shown in practicing dentistry and relying on a colleague or mentor for expertise in a procedure. It also can go in his business practice in asking someone like me to help build his practice.

**5. Confident dentists strive to grow their practice.**

A confident dentist doesn't restrict how big his practice can get. This means there are no limits to how much success the confident dentist sees for himself.

6. **Confident dentists don't have to put others down to lift themselves up.**

   This, like many others on this list, extends beyond dentists. Tearing down other people, whether that is competitors, acquaintances, or whomever, doesn't build anyone up. Confident dentists don't need to do so.

7. **Confident dentists aren't afraid to be themselves.**

   I see this in video especially. We want dentists to be themselves on camera so that patients get to know them. But some dentists want to put on a persona to be more professional or serious. Confident dentists are comfortable being who they are. Being yourself is a great way to attract patients that you will mesh with.

8. **Confident dentists own their mistakes.**

   A confident dentist knows that we are not defined by our mistakes. Being wrong about a treatment option or a business decision does not cost a dentist esteem. Acting like he wasn't wrong costs a dentist esteem. A confident dentist knows that he gains esteem by acknowledging he was wrong and making it right.

9. **Finally, confident dentists see challenges as opportunities.**

   A confident dentist knows he has the talent to be a good dentist. He just needs to get the right combination of ingredients to get his practice go-ing. This confidence comes from his willingness to change and adapt his practice to better attract patients.

Are you a confident dentist? If so, I would love to work with you.

**COLIN RECEVEUR**, a nationally recognized dental marketing expert and speaker, is the author of several books on internet marketing, including *The Four Horsemen of Dentistry: Survival Strategies for the Private Dental Practice Under Siege*. His company, SmartBox, helps more than 550 dentists on three continents get more patients, more profits, and more freedom.